Prosperity Magic

Spell Working for Abundance, Money, and Prosperity

Prosperity Magic

Spell Working for Abundance, Money, and Prosperity

Rachel Patterson

MOON BOOKS
London, UK
Washington, DC, USA

CollectiveInk

First published by Moon Books, 2025
Moon Books is an imprint of Collective Ink Ltd.,
Unit 11, Shepperton House, 89 Shepperton Road, London, N1 3DF
office@collectiveinkbooks.com
www.collectiveinkbooks.com
www.moon-books.net

For distributor details and how to order please visit the 'Ordering' section on our website.

ISBN: 978 1 80341 976 3
978 1 80341 727 1 (ebook)
Library of Congress Control Number: 2024948594

A CIP catalogue record for this book is available from the British Library.

Design: Lapiz Digital Services
Illustrated by Kay Savage

UK: Printed and bound by CPI Group (UK) Ltd, Croydon, CR0 4YY
US: Printed and bound by Thomson-Shore, 7300 West Joy Road, Dexter, MI 48130

CONTENTS

Introduction

I have been writing the 'Witch that gets you rich' column for *Fate and Fortune* magazine since 2019 so I have a lot of prosperity magic experience, it made sense to bring it all together to form this book.

Welcome to the realm of money-making magic, but just a reminder that prosperity and abundance don't just arrive in monetary form. You can manifest abundance into your life in all kinds of ways, it might be an abundance of love and happiness. It could be an abundance of good friends or neighbours. You might even like to manifest an abundance of furry four-legged friends too. Whilst money is sadly a necessity in this modern fast paced world, it is nothing without an abundance of love and positive vibes.

It is also worth remembering that nothing comes for free. Even with spell working there is always a price to pay, spell working involves a system of checks and balances. You cannot keep asking for things from deity, the divine, the universe, whoever you call upon without giving something back, that's not how it works. Offerings need to be made in exchange, whether that is in the form of food or plant matter on your altar, feeding the birds, clearing up rubbish in your neighbourhood or just giving some of your own time to help out a neighbour. An offering must be made for each request.

Think also about gratitude, you have asked for something, so it is only fair and actually just plain good manners to give thanks for what you receive. But also give a thought to what you already have. It might not be exactly what you believe you need or deserve, but there will be lots of things in your life to already be grateful for. That being said, never believe that you are not worthy of asking for a little prosperity to come your way, because you totally are.

Prosperity magic also covers releasing yourself from debts, so I have included spell working for that purpose too.

Within this book you will find a whole host of spells to work to bring prosperity and abundance into your life. Work them as they are or tweak them to suit your needs or what you have to hand and personalise them to suit you.

You will also find information on areas of prosperity magic and some hints and tips to short and quick methods to work with.

A Note on currency: As I live in the UK, the currency I refer to are pennies and pounds. If you are reading this elsewhere in the world just translate my currency to yours… cents, dollars and euros are every bit as magical!

Setting the Scene

Spell working can be as simple as staring up at the moon and telling her your needs through to a full-on elaborate ritual with all the bells and whistles. I like to work magic somewhere in between. I think spell working should be kept simple, anything more complicated has a far greater chance of going awry. Don't get me wrong, spells do go off in unexpected directions on occasion, you need to trust that the universe knows what it is doing. Always remember 'what you want isn't always what you need'. Be clear with your requests, be strong with your will and intent, if you put effort into it your spell will have a greater chance of working out well.

Adding in herbs, colours and other ingredients to your spells adds layers of extra power to them, as does working them on corresponding moon or sun phases. Take your time to plan out your spell working properly and in detail. Each of your ingredients will need charging before you add them to your spell, send the energy and intent into them.

Always remember to give thanks when asking for something, offerings can be simple such as pouring water onto the ground, feeding the birds or leaving an offering of fresh flowers for the Gods.

Take responsibility for the magic that you put out there. Spell working is about transformation, you are manipulating energy to change things to go your way, you need to take responsibility for those changes. There is no spell that is totally selfless. Whatever magic you work will have an effect on someone somewhere, that's how spells work. I am not trying to dissuade you from working them, absolutely not, just be mindful that you own that spell and stand by it.

There is no shortcut to experience with spell working, the only way to learn how they work and to improve on them is to do it. If you are new to spell working, I would advise keeping a detailed record, note down what you use, what you say, how you work it and any correspondences. This way you can refer back to it once the spell has been actioned and see what worked or what didn't. You learn from each experience.

Work within your budget, spell working should not be expensive. Check your kitchen cupboards, your garden or in nature for ingredients. You don't need to order exotic expensive ingredients to be shipped across the globe. In fact, I firmly believe ingredients sourced locally will work much better as you will have a personal connection to them.

Take your time, enjoy the process and reap the rewards, you are worth it.

General Magic Suggestions

This section of the book covers general ideas for working prosperity magic. They are ideas and experiences that I have worked with over the years that you can use to create your own spells or just little rituals that can be carried out to help boost abundance in your life.

A Prosperity Altar

Anyone can have an altar, or a sacred space dedicated to a particular intent. Having a prosperity altar can really help keep the money coming in and it doesn't have to be a huge space. A small shelf or top of a side table would work perfectly. It also doesn't need to look like an altar and by that, I mean it can blend in with your furnishings and not be 'obviously' magical. Find a space that suits you and put a cloth over it. You might want to purchase a small tablecloth especially for it but a 'fat quarter' of material from a fabric store, an old scarf or tablecloth will work just as well. If you can use one that is green, gold or orange in colour then you bring in prosperity, wealth and success with colour magic.

Now think about what you would like to put on the altar, these will be items that you associate with prosperity, money, luck or success. Have a look around your home and see what you already have there. My suggestions would be:

- A green, gold or orange candle in a holder.
- A few silver or gold coins.
- A small vase with fresh greenery.
- An old purse or wallet.
- Crystals that you associate with money such as malachite or green aventurine.
- Herbs you associate with money such as mint or basil.
- A money box or piggy bank.

As you place each item onto the altar charge it with your intent. Hold the item in your hands and visualise money coming to you. You might like to say something such as:

"With this item I do say
Money and prosperity will come my way
On my prosperity altar you will stay
Luck and success roll in from this day"

Place the items where you think they need to be, make a nice display.

Each day you can light the candle and visualise money coming to you. You may also want to add a little dish as an offering plate. Pop a few herbs, seeds or coins into the dish every so often as an offering and a thanks to the divine.

If you have any bills that arrive, fold them up and place them on the altar with the intent that money will arrive to cover the amount.

Keep the altar clean, dusted and fresh to keep the prosperity magic working.

A Prosperous You

What we wear and put on our bodies can affect prosperity magic. Have a think about when you get dressed and what items could bring in a little more luck and wealth.

Green items of clothing or those with gold or silver buttons on can bring money your way. Orange clothing stands for success and gold is a definite signal for wealth to find its way to you. Say a little magic when you get dressed, perhaps something along the lines of:

"With the magic of what I wear
Prosperity and money will fill the air
My clothing attracts money to me
The fabric brings wealth for me to see".

Your shoes can walk money with each step, sprinkle some dried mint inside your shoes or draw a £ or $ sign on the sole of your shoes to bring money to you.

Jewellery can also bring in the dosh. Charge a pendant, bracelet or ring with the intent of drawing money towards you. Hold the item in your hand and say:

"The sparkle of silver and gold

Will bring money for me to behold
Metal to attract the shine
Prosperity and wealth will be mine"

Wear the item as you go out and about. If you wear make-up you can charge any of it to bring prosperity your way. Hold the item in your hand and visualise money coming to you, then put on your lipstick or eyeliner ready to take on the day. You can synch your colours for money power. Green or gold eyeshadow will bring prosperity and red lipstick is a 'go get 'em' power colour. Paint your nails in a green, gold or orange and add plenty of sparkle to help draw money into your hands. You could even paint small £ or $ signs onto each nail.

Fashion Manifesting

Think about the colours you wear and the items of clothing and how they can be used for abundance and prosperity magic.

Buttons – symbolize bringing things together, keeping things together or tying up a situation, this can apply perfectly to your finances. If your garment has buttons on, as you do the buttons up see your finances coming together in a positive way, for each button say:

"As I button up, bring prosperity my way"

If like me, you have a jar of odd buttons these can be used for money magic. Pick a button that represents the colour of money, you might like to choose a green or gold one. Hold the button in your hand and charge it with the intent of bringing money in. Say:

"Button magic bring money to me
Button magic charged for prosperity
Pop the button in your purse or bag."

Buttons bind things together so you can also use them to curb your spending habits. As you button up your garment say:

"Buttons done up to stop the spend
Buttons done up my finances to mend"

If you have some loose buttons, pick one that represents money to you, a green or gold one would work well. Hold the button in your hand and charge it with the intent of curbing your spending habits. You might say:

"Button magic help with my finances and mend
Button magic help me stop and think before I spend"

Pop the button in your purse or wallet.

I love to work with colour magic and that extends to your clothing. Choose colours that represent money, prosperity and abundance. I associate the colours of green, gold and silver with money and prosperity. In ancient Rome only those who were rich would wear the colour purple as it was expensive to produce, so that may be your abundance colour of choice. Wear an item of clothing in that colour, it could just be a scarf or gloves, it will bring you luck and abundance for the day.

If you wear a belt you can draw a symbol on the reverse side that represents money and prosperity, I would suggest a pound £ sign. Once you have drawn the symbol hold the belt and visualize money coming to you and new financial opportunities opening up. Put the belt on and as you do up the buckle say:

"Power of prosperity magic bring money to me
Buckle up with new opportunities for me to see"

Draw prosperity symbols such as pound signs on the soles of your shoes (inside or underneath). Charge it with the intent of bringing money and new opportunities to you as you walk. Say:

"With each step I take
More and more money I will make"

Body Oil

Body oils can also be made and used to anoint your head and wrists or used on your full body as you would a body moisturiser. Please do a skin test patch before you go sloshing a whole load of body oil blend on, just in case you are allergic to any of the ingredients! You can also charge your perfume or usual body moisturiser with prosperity energy.

Fast Money Body Oil Blend:

Massage into the skin or add to your pulse points to become a money magnet.
You will need:

3 tablespoons base oil such as almond, coconut, sunflower or jojoba
10 drops mint essential oil
5 drops vanilla essential oil
5 drops frankincense essential oil

Mix the oils together. Store in an airtight bottle for up to three months.

Manifesting Magic Screen

These suggestions all work whether you are using a mobile phone or tablet home or lock screen or on a laptop or PC, the premise is the same. It is a visual aid to help your money-making magic, literally a spell on a screen.

I often put an image on the home or lock screen of my mobile or PC of something I wish to manifest, bring into my life or speed up. It means I see the image on a regular basis and can add some visualisation energy to the 'spell' to boost the power. Images are easy to download from the internet to use.

Here are some suggestions of images to use:

- Money – this one is perhaps obvious. Use an image of piles of cash, notes or coins it doesn't matter. The idea is to give the image of lots of lovely money.
- Treasure – think pirate or dragon hoards and you will be on the right track. Gold, silver, precious metals and jewels, crowns, tiaras and sceptres of all kinds. Make it sparkly and shiny.
- Car – need cash for a new car? Pop an image of the car you would like to get your hands on up on your screen. Obviously keep it real, putting up an image of a fancy limited edition James Bond carriage will be a bit of a stretch for magic to obtain for you (unless of course you have that sort of money lying around). Keep it practical and put an image up of a car that you need, something that is within the realms of possibility.
- Holiday – want to gather some money together to go on holiday? Pop up a picture of the country, town, city or landscape you would like to visit.
- Furniture – perhaps you are after a new sofa, table or bed. Find an image of the item you desire and pop it up on your screen.
- Kitchen/Bathroom – is your home in need of a kitchen or bathroom makeover? Find an image of something you like and get that up on your screen pronto.

- Shoes – who doesn't love new shoes? Or clothing or any kind, you could even put together a collage of different items you would like to manifest.

This idea works for whatever you want to manifest, just find an image of what it is you are seeking and add it to your screen. Once you have uploaded your image to the screen, set the intent in motion. You could say a little chant, something along the lines of:

"Manifesting magic, see my spell upon the screen
Unfold my desires and don't be mean
Techno power bring these things to me
By the power and boost of electricity"

Repeat this chant on a regular basis, perhaps once a day when you first look at your screen during the day until the magic has worked.

Phone Magic Manifesting

Our mobile phones have become an integral part of our daily lives, and they provide a good connection to the world around us. But how about using them to work some manifesting magic?

Here are my ideas:

- Vision Board - I often put an image on the home or lock screen of something I want to happen, bring into my life or speed up. It means I see it often and add my energy to the 'spell' to boost it. I took this idea a step further and decided to use a vision board and use the image on my phone home screen. If you need money fast you could use an image of cash. In need of a dream vacation? Pop an image of the place you would like to visit on your homes screen. What about a new car or new house – save an image from the internet of the item you desire and pop it on your phone. Each time you use your phone add a bit of positive energy to the image.

- Music – When you are working a magical spell to bring money your way how about boosting the energy by playing a song that links to prosperity? Look for a song with money or cash in the title and/or in the words. Play it from your phone as you work the spell.
- Moon Phases – there are a huge number of moon phase apps available to download for free to your mobile phone. You can use these to check the correct moon phase to use when working magic for prosperity and abundance. New, waxing and full moon phases are best for drawing money to you. Work with the waning moon phases to release your debts.
- Crystal apps – there are some good crystal apps available to download, these can be used to recommend the best crystals to work with for prosperity and abundance.
- Tarot/Oracle – you will find a variety of tarot or oracle card apps free to download. These can be used for daily card pulls without the need of a deck of your own. Ask questions about your finances and click to select a card for advice and insight.
- Meditation – you are spoilt for choice when it comes to apps for meditation to download. If you search you can find some that are specifically for manifesting or drawing money to you.

Household Magic for Manifesting

There are lots of things within the house that can be used for manifesting money, abundance and prosperity. Some of these come to us from folk lore, others just make magical sense. Have a walk around your home and see what items you associated with money and think about how you could work some magic with them.

Here are some of my suggestions:

- Place a silver coin under your front doormat to keep money coming into the home.
- Keep a jar of spare change by the front door this helps keep prosperity coming into the house.
- Place a mirror on the wall near the centre of a room, it rings good luck.
- Hang a mirror over a doorway to bless those who enter.
- Pop a spare green or gold coloured button in your purse to work some colour magic, to bring prosperity.
- Keep a button in the drawer with your bank statements to keep your finances 'together'.
- Folklore says that if you make a wish on a button and then throw it in a well the Fairies will be happy and will grant your wish.
- Folklore says that gifting buttons to newlyweds brought about luck. In fact, gifting buttons to anyone seems to be a lucky thing, give it a try!
- Looking to raise some cash, how about putting on some music when you are in the home that relates to money. Think about the title or lyrics of a song and if it mentions lots of cash, play it loud!
- If you take a bath, when you are finished and pull the plug out, visualise all your debts being washed down the drain with the water.
- Use your shower gel to draw a £ symbol on your skin before you wash it away in the shower.
- Write the amount of your debt on a piece of toilet paper and flush it down the loo.

- Use shaving foam to draw money symbols on the bathroom tiles before you clean them.
- Your purse, wallet or handbag is literally a money spell pouch. Dab mint oil inside or pop a dried basil or mint leaf inside to bring prosperity in. Draw the infinity symbol inside your purse to keep money coming in continuously.
- Keys are a symbol of unlocking new avenues of opportunity, if you have an old key, charge it with the energy of opening new money-making ventures and pop it in your purse or bag.
- As you wash and peel vegetables visualise your debts being washed away with the soil and outer peel.
- When you dust and polish your home, see the dust as being negative energy and debts that you are banishing away. As you bring in the polish see it as positive abundant energy.
- Pop a crystal on top of your wifi router to bring in abundance, something like a piece of green aventurine that will work prosperity magic as your wifi sends the signal around the house.
- Write pound signs on the reverse of your door mats.

With all of these suggestions, set the magic in motion by stating your intent out loud as you action them. Tell the universe the purpose is to bring abundance and prosperity your way. It helps to visualise your goal at the same time.

Bringing Money into Your Home

Take three silver coins, all the same size. Write the words 'prosperity, abundance and wealth' on a slip of paper. Place the coins, all heads up on top of each other and wrap them in the paper. If you want to add to the magic, you could use green paper or tie the paper up with green string or ribbon. Pop your little money parcel under the front door mat to your home. Each time a person steps over your threshold they will bring abundance and prosperity into your home with them.

Tie a bunch of herbs with green ribbon or twine and hang it over the doorframe to your front door, this will bring luck and prosperity into your home. Use whatever herbs you have to hand but basil and mint work well.

Tie cinnamon sticks with a red ribbon and place them in your porch or just inside the front door to your home to bring in positive successful energy.

Money Washes

Spiritual folk have used washes as a way of cleansing both the body and the soul for centuries, these spiritual washes can be used in the bath, shower and also to wash the house, home and floors. The herbs and roots are steeped in water and then sieved. I find it easier to use herbal tea bags.

Floor washes are used for all sorts of purposes – mopping the floor to bring in good fortune and luck or to wash away negative energies and evil in the main but can also be used for any intent.

There is a process to follow: when you want to clean your house in the spiritual removing negative energy (and actually as a by-product in the physical) you start from the top of the building and work your way down, also working from the back of the house to the front, finishing up on your front doorstep. To bring positive energy and prosperity to your home you should make sure your front doorstep is scrubbed clean, work inwards towards the home.

For ritual bathing of yourself it works best if you wash yourself upwards to bring good fortune and downwards to dispel negativity.

Any water that has been used for spiritual cleansing should be disposed of by throwing it away to the east, preferably before the sun rises. You don't have to lug bucketfuls of your used bathwater all the way outside to do this you can use a small amount as a 'token'.

Lucky Money Wash Recipe

You will need:

2 tablespoons dried mint (or you could use a couple of peppermint tea bags)
3 cups water

- Steep the teabags or dried mint in hot water for 10 minutes. Strain and store it in an airtight bottle or a spritzer.
- Pour a small amount into your palms and 'wash' your hands with it or using the spritzer, spray your hands to bring you luck.
- Add a splash to your bath water for an abundance bath.
- Dab a small amount on your money to keep it coming in.
- Pop a drop inside your purse or wallet to bring money to you.
- To use as a floor wash; drop the teabags or herbs straight into a bucket of warm water and use a mop to bring prosperity to your home.
- Dip a cloth in the herb wash and wipe down all your surfaces and window frames to bring prosperity in.

Wash Away Debts

Rain is by its very nature a cleansing element. We can tap into this power by using rain to literally wash away any debts that we might have.

The simplest rain spell is to take your credit card or loan statement and leave it out in the rain.

Lay the paper out flat and secure it with a couple of pebbles. Please make sure this is in a safe place such as your own garden. As you pin the paper out, visualize your debts disappearing and money coming in that will enable you to pay off anything you owe. Don't just see the lottery paying out, because that only happens to a few people! See the universe providing you with the means to earn more or a bonus coming your way. Allow the rain to really soak the paper until it starts to break up.

An alternative is to write the amount of money you owe on a slip of paper and follow the same process.

You can also just draw the amount in the dirt in your garden. Clear a space and flatten the soil, then scratch the number into the dirt. When it rains it will wash the figures away and hopefully your debts with it.

A Wishing Board

This spell work uses visual aids, sometimes referred to as a vision board. It is perfect to manifest something like a holiday because you can use images from postcards or travel brochures, along with any odd foreign cash. But the idea can be utilised for all sorts of intents. Perhaps you want to manifest a new car, a new job, some new furniture or just good old cash. The wishing/vision board is where the magic happens.

You will need:

A cork notice board, magnetic white board or use PowerPoint or an online app such as Pinterest.

Images of the items you want to manifest – photos, postcards, pictures printed from the internet, magazine or leaflet images, foreign currency, toy money – the list is endless

Magnets or drawing pins

Set the board in front of you (or your computer screen) now decide what your main goal is. It might be bringing money in or something specific such as a holiday. Let's work with a holiday as an example. Perhaps you would like to go on holiday to Greece. You need to look for images of places you would like to visit in Greece and print them off or cut them out of travel brochures. Also, images of restaurants in Greece, or photos of delicious Greek food and glasses of wine. Perhaps an image of an aeroplane as well. You could add a picture of a suitcase, sun hat and sunglasses or sunny beach photos. If you have any currency, you could pop that on there too, or print off an image from the internet.

Get your images all cut out and ready and set them in front of you. Now make your statement to the Universe out loud:

"My desire, I wish to manifest, a holiday to Greece, to relax and rest"

Next start adding your images to your board, in any order or layout that you feel is right. Keep repeating the chant as you add each image. When you are finished say the chant out loud a final time and finish it with 'so mote it be'.

Place the board somewhere prominent where you will see it regularly. Every few days stop in front of the board and say the chant again.

Then when the time is right...pack your suitcase!

Abundance Mandala

You will need:

- Crystals
- Pebbles
- Candle
- Tarot cards
- Leaves
- Herbs
- Flowers
- Whatever you like!

I don't really have a proper name for this type of creation – power wheel, medicine wheel, mandala…you may feel the need to call it something completely different but whatever the name of it this wheel is a powerful source of energy to be directed to whatever intent you feel the need for. It is like a big visual spell.

I like to start with a central feature whether it is a crystal, a pebble, a candle or a tarot card of some sort – it gives the focus of intent. I then fan out in circles (or you could spiral it) using whatever I am drawn to use. Your intent is to bring things towards you (money and prosperity) so place the items in the circle in a clockwise way.

You can use all natural items such as pebbles, shells, leaves, sticks and flowers if you want to keep it totally wild. However, you can add in crystals or tarot and oracle cards if you like to use them.

Be creative and go with what works for you! I have seen mandalas created with coffee pods and staplers! Once your mandala is created visualize the outcome, see money and abundance coming your way.

I leave the wheel creations in place for as long as feels necessary, sometimes the wind will blow the parts around if I have created it outside. Once the wind has done its work it usually feels like the right time to dismantle it. Otherwise, it gets left alone until I feel the wheel has done the work required.

If I have used cards and crystals, they get cleansed and put away the rest gets put into the compost bin, recycling or buried. Never leave anything outside that won't degrade properly.

Money-Making Symbols

The most obvious symbol to use for money making is the pound sign but you can also use the dollar sign or any of the currency symbols.

Did you know there is also a currency symbol for unspecified currency. This one is useful if you are working magic to draw money to you from various countries or sources. Using this doesn't narrow down your options for money sources. The symbol is a small circle with four short arms that radiate around it, the sign is sometimes referred to as a scarab, it does look a little like a beetle!

The infinity symbol can also be used, it looks like the figure 8 laying on its side. This can symbolise a never-ending source of money.

The circle is a simple sign to use when working money drawing magic, it has no end, so it works perfectly to draw a money avenue to you that is indefinite.

Alchemy symbols are also useful, for instance the sign for gold is a circle with a dot in the centre or you could use the letters 'Au'. Silver is represented by the letters 'Ag' and is often seen as three arrows pointing upwards.

Abundance and prosperity are often shown using a simple image of a wheat sheaf or the cornucopia. The rune symbol for wealth is Fehu, it looks similar to a capital letter F. A simple fish shape is also representative of prosperity.

Any of these symbols can be used magically to bring money, prosperity and abundance your way.

- Draw your symbol on the bottom of your shoe, as you take steps you literally 'walk' money your way.
- Draw the symbol inside your purse or wallet.
- Paint the symbols on your nails with nail varnish.
- Discreetly pencil the symbols on the back of invoices or proposals you send to new customers.
- Draw the symbols in the air before you step into a meeting or a visit to the bank.
- Trace the symbol with your finger on the front of your lottery ticket before you submit it.
- Draw the symbol in the sand on the beach or the earth in your garden.
- Visualise the symbol on any surface or in any situation to help boost your finances.

The options for using these symbols whether drawn with pen, pencil, paint or your finger in the air are limitless.

Solar Symbols to Increase Your Cash

There are various symbols and images which have been and are associated with the sun or solar energy. They can be placed on your around your home in honour of solar energy or the sun gods, drawn on petition papers or inscribed into candles for candle magic. Each one carries the power of the sun for growth, financial stability, prosperity and abundance. Here are some of the more recognised ones:

Triskelion – This three-legged sign is thought to represent the sun in its stages of sunrise, midday and sunset. It also represents the triple goddess, the three worlds (living, dead and spirit) and the stages of life. It can be used to bring money and prosperity into your life.

Swastika – Oh, this is such a misused and misunderstood symbol when really its original meaning is full of beauty. It actually faces the opposite way to the Nazi use of the symbol; you often see it in Hindu and Buddhist temples. It is a symbol of the sun and stands for prosperity, eternity, abundance and good fortune.

Sun cross – Basically, a circle with an equilateral cross inside it. This symbol was found throughout ancient cultures and is believed to have been a solar symbol. The term 'sun cross' seems to be more modern but the image of a cross in a circle has very ancient roots, thought to symbolise the wheel of the sun god's chariot. The cross represents the four compass directions: north, east, south and west. The circle is a whole and can symbolise you or your family and this symbol can be used to draw money quickly to you.

Spiral – This is such a simple image but one of my favourites. It symbolises life, rebirth, growth, connection to the divine, consciousness, creation and spirituality. It can lead from the material world round into the inner spirit. The spiral can be used to draw money and prosperity to you.

Circle – Basic but brilliant. The circle is round like the sun and never ending like the sun (well obviously it does have a shelf life but hopefully it will last us a few more millennia!). Circles represent the planet and if you get the colour right (yellow or gold) it makes an excellent representation of the sun. It is a symbol of wholeness, everything, perfection, infinity, cycles, revolution, centring and completion. The circle can be drawn to bring prosperity and abundance to you but also to increase growth of your finances.

Wheel – Not only does the wheel have a connection to all the sun gods and their chariots (chariots needing wheels of course), but it is also a circle. It goes around...and round...as does the sun and the cycle of life. A brilliant symbol to use to bring money to you when you need it really quickly.

Infinity – The infinity symbol which looks like a figure '8' laid on its side is never ending, hence being called 'infinity'. There is an astronomical situation where the position of the sun is traced in the sky throughout an entire year, seen from a fixed point. When you map the journey of the sun you get the infinity symbol. Perfect to draw on the back of cheques or spells to keep the money come in 'to infinity and beyond'.

Word Spells

Successful spell work is based on several ingredients. Your intent needs to be strong and focused and your will to reach your goal should be honed. You can use candles, herbs, oils and crystals along with planetary phases and alignments to add layers of energy. But here's the thing, sometimes simple is best and a well-tuned verse or chant can bring about prosperity and abundance without the need for all the bells and whistles. You also don't need to be an accomplished poet, particularly with modern access to Thesaurus and rhyming dictionaries on the internet. Write yourself a simple verse or chant and say it out loud. I like to repeat a chant a certain number of times to raise the energy of it. Three times is good, six times gets the energy going and nine times is a serious amount of magical energy. Then you release that magic into the universe for it to do its thing.

Let's look at rhyming, this works because it follows an almost melodic pattern. For prosperity spell verses think about words such as prosperity (obviously), money, abundance, cash and wealth.

Rhyming words might be:

> Prosperity – me, see, free, thee, be, charity, austerity, sincerity

Cash – flash, brash, crash, dash, stash, lash, smash
Wealth – stealth, health

Abundance and money are difficult ones to rhyme, so I tend to lean towards including them within the sentence rather than at the end! Me is a good one to end with as it rhymes with things like be, free, see, spree, thee, we, decree and foresee.

Here are some examples:

"Universe, I ask of thee,
Bring abundance and prosperity to me"

Or

"Grant to me to cover my debt
As I ask for money, so it is met"

Or

"I ask that money and enough cash
Comes direct to me and in a flash"

Your words don't need to rhyme, but they should flow as it helps build the energy. Try using alliteration instead, using words such as:

Cash, come, create and credit
Money, make, most, met, more, massive
Abundance, amazing, amounts, ask, access

An example might be

"Credit me with cash, may it come to me"

Or

"I ask for amazing amounts of abundance now"

Create your verse and repeat it each morning and night, visualizing money coming to you, until it takes effect.

Knot and Cord Magic

The use of cords and knots for magical purpose is an old one but it is still a very useful form of magic today. Knot and cord magic is simple, uses simple items, magic can be achieved by using a piece of string! It is also incredibly powerful and can be worked in plain sight with no one having any idea you are working magic. You can use a piece of string, but it could also be ribbon, wool or twine, in fact anything that you can tie, even your shoelaces can be used for magical purpose.

- Cutting the cord can be used as a simple but effective means of releasing yourself from debt or a bad cycle in life.
- Knots can be tied into string to bring money in or secure your finances.

So many uses for a simple piece of string. Tying a knot helps keep something secure and safe, untying a knot or cutting the string releases and let's go.

It is a perfect and easy form of magic.

Prosperity Weather Magic

The power of wind is extremely strong, even the slightest breeze can be used to blow away negative energy, vibes or bad debts. If you find yourself in a storm situation you will be able to harness some really powerful wind magic.

Storms whip up a super charged amount of energy so if you know one is coming then you could work your money magic while the storm is raging. It will boost your prosperity energy.

The simplest abundance wind spell is to tell the wind what you need. Whisper an amount or your monetary request to the gentle breeze or shout it into the storm. Like snow and water, the wind has a talent for transformation. Draw on that power to transform your finances.

- If the wind is blowing in from the East, it brings extra magic of renewal and new beginnings.
- Wind from the south is one of action and fiery energy.
- West winds bring strength, cleansing and the fertility of new ideas and ventures.
- The North wind brings changes and is the best wind to work with for material gain, money and prosperity.

If you have a layer of fallen snow you can write wishes and money symbols into the snow. Draw a pound or dollar sign or write an amount of money into the snow. As it melts it will work its prosperity magic.

If you want to release yourself from a debt, make a snowball and send the intent into the snowball to remove your debt. Then throw the snowball as far away as you can.

Rain can wash away debts. Write the amount of your debt in the soil in your garden and allow the rain to wash it away. Alternatively write the amount on a piece of paper and peg it out in the pouring rain to allow the water to wash away the writing, taking the debt with it.

Snow and Ice Money Magic

Basically, snow and ice are variations on frozen water, so they are water in a transformed state which brings the energy of transformation.

When you collect your snow, it will also change the energy, for instance if you scoop up a handful of the white stuff when fresh snow has laid and the land is still and silent it can be used in spell work for calming tempers or soothing situations. If you collect snow during a raging blizzard then it will pack a huge powerful punch of energy.

If you are tempted out into the snow, once you have finished your snowball fight how about building snow shapes and carving pound signs into them?

- If you want to get rid of a bad debt, write the amount on a slip of paper and bury it in the snow. As the snow melts it takes away the debt with it.
- You can also write your wishes and goals in the snow, as it melts your intent is released to the universe. Write a sum of money or just lots of pound signs in the snow with your finger.
- Another way to get rid of bad debts is to dump that energy into a snowball and throw it away from you as far as you can.
- Collect a jar full of snow and once it has melted use it as 'snow water'. The same can be done with ice or icicles, pop them in a jar to melt. The water can be used later on to dissolve debts.

Solar Water Magic

Solar water carries the magic of prosperity and growth so it will aid your finances. Try sprinkling some solar water on your money before you put it into your purse. Or washing your hands in solar water before you fill in your lottery ticket numbers. It can be used to water your plants that need a bit of a boost, to sprinkle on your spell work to boost the energy, drink a sip when you need an energy lift, before you work magic or just before doing your accounts or seeing your bank manager. Add it to your baking or cooking to send in the magic or pop a bit into your bathwater.

And it is really easy to make:

- Solstice water – Set out a jar or dish of water during the solstice and let it soak up the energy. Then you can bottle it and use it at a later date.
- Sunrise/midday/sunset – Set your jar of water out during the phase of the sun you want to capture. Bottle it and use at a later date for the intent that corresponds to the phase you used to charge it under.
- Solar water – for general purpose sun water, set out a dish or jar of water first thing in the morning and allow it to soak up the energy from the sun throughout the day. Take it in at sunset.

Obviously make sure your jar or dish of water is covered so that you don't end up with fly water...yuck!

Sand Spells

Sand is a wonderful medium to use for writing wishes to increase your prosperity and abundance or to remove debts with the power of the ocean. The tides bring changes and represent the ever-changing cycle of life, it is cleansing and brings growth and new pathways and opportunities.

The sand is also representative of all the elements, the earth, the ocean, the wind and the sun.

There are also millions and millions of grains of sand which is a good correspondence for abundance!

Stand just back from the water's edge and find a flat piece of sand. Now write with your finger or your spade in the sand. Keep it short and simple. You may want to use one of the solar symbols we have included here, or just a pound sign would work well too. Writing the word 'money' or 'prosperity' is also a good option. Don't make it too complicated. As you write your word or draw your symbol in the sand visualise the money rolling in. You could also add shells or pebbles to your design. Visualising your intent as you do so. Then leave it. Allow the sun to shine upon your wish and then at some point during the day the tide will come in and wash away the drawing, as it does so the magic is released and begins to work. If you want the ocean to release your debt, then writing the word 'debts' in the sand works well too.

It's a Numbers Game

How do you work with these numbers to boost your finances?

- Write the number 6 or 8 inside your wallet or purse.
- Write the number 6 on the sole of your left shoe and the number 8 on the sole of your right shoe, to create prosperity as you walk.
- Draw the number 6 or 8 under your front door mat.
- Trace the number 6 or 8 in the palm of your hand before you pay for something, make a bet or write a lottery ticket.
- Keep 6 coins in your purse to keep the money coming in.
- Repeat chants in spell working 6 or 8 times.
- Carve the number 6 or 8 into a candle before working a money spell.
- Write the amount of money you need 6 or 8 times on a petition slip for spell work.
- Use 6 or 8 ingredients in a money-making spell pouch.

Money Magic Garden

You could create areas in your garden that are specifically for prosperity and abundance. As each plant has one or more magical properties (usually several) you can grow plants as individual spells or create an entire bed with a specific intent. Seeds also work well as growing spells. Plant the seed with your intent and then add your energy to it each day to keep the spell going.

A prosperity garden might include lots of green foliage, green being a colour of money. Add in orange flowers for success and maybe plants that have lots of seeds such as fennel, seeds being good for prosperity. Grow plants that are associated with the magical correspondences of money and prosperity such as:

> Ash, basil, bergamot (orange), calamus, camellia, cedar, chamomile, clover, comfrey, dill, dock, fenugreek, ginger, goldenrod, gorse, hazel, honeysuckle, honesty, jasmine, mandrake, mint, myrtle, nettle, oak, patchouli, periwinkle, poppy, skullcap, tulip, vervain and woodruff.

If you don't have room for a prosperity flower bed, then just plan a few pots specifically with prosperity plants in. If you don't have a garden, how about a pot plant on your windowsill with a prosperity magic plant in?

Add to the money magic by drawing pound signs on the plant pots or popping a silver coin in the soil before you plant the seeds or plants in the earth.

As you plant each one you could also chant:

"With the element of earth as I plant
Money, wealth and prosperity I chant
Bring these things to me as the plants grow
Make it count, a really great big show"

Spring Flower Magic

In April the garden begins to come alive, and lots of spring plants carry money magic or the ability to create new projects or ventures with them. Let's have a look at two of the favourites. You can grow them in your garden or keep a pot of the flowers on a windowsill indoors to bring the magic into your life.

Daffodil - (*Narcissus spp*) – Daffodils are one of my favourite flowers, such a welcome sight after the darkness of winter. Daffodil brings with it the magic of rebirth so is excellent to use in fertility workings and that doesn't just mean the babies kind. Fertility can be new ideas, new projects, ventures or possibilities for earning money and bringing in new sources of cash. Have daffodils growing in your garden to bring protection to your house and also to clear out negative energies, also good to use in workings to remove negative spells. Having daffodils in the house brings luck, love and blessings to your home.

Crocus - (*Crocus vemus*) – Often one of the first signs that spring is on the way, these pretty little flowers grow in woodlands, meadows and are cultivated in gardens. The crocus brings with it the promise of spring, new projects, new ideas and new ventures and if you are looking for it – new love. Grow crocus in your garden or bring a bowl of crocus indoors to promote love in your home. Keep a pot of crocus by your front door and they will bring happiness and hope to your house. Visualise crocus or hold a crocus when you meditate and allow the spirit of the plant to take you on a journey and share its knowledge and wisdom with you via visions.

Flower Divination

Divination with natural objects such as flowers and plants can be an interesting project to delve into. We can use plant divination to take a peek into your financial situation and gain advice and insight.

Botomancy is divination using plants.
Floromancy is divination using flowers.

Once you get to know your garden you will begin to understand what is usual and what isn't. Differences in how a plant looks and grows or how the wildlife acts can be taken as a sign or message. But you can also use plant items specifically for divination.

- You can make lovely pendulums with flower heads just tie one onto the end of a piece of thread and use it as you would with any pendulum.
- Stems from tall plants such as yarrow or chives can be used in a system like iChing.
- Flowers, herbs and seed heads can be floated on the surface of water for scrying.
- Burning herbs and leaves to read the smoke for messages.
- Pop some bay leaves onto charcoal or an open fire and visualise your question. If the leaves burn with a bright flame and crackle loudly then the answer is positive, if they fizzle out and smoulder sadly then the answer is no.
- Create a divination set using dried seed and flower heads to cast as you would with runes.
- Press flowers and leaves and stick them to card to create your own oracle deck.
- Vervain, fig and sycamore leaves are particular favourites for using in Botomancy. Plants that have showy flowers, spikes or thorns are especially good.
- Plants can be thrown on the fire and then the smoke or the ashes are read. Sometimes a question or symbols to represent a question are carved on the branches before burning them.

- Words written on leaves especially those of the fig and sage can be released to the wind. The leaves that are not blown away revealed the answer to a question.

Folklore has its fair share of flower and plant divination: The first flower that appears in your garden has a meaning, depending on what day of the week it arrives.

Monday – brings good fortune
Tuesday – assures success in your ventures
Wednesday – brings marriage or a partnership
Thursday – a bit of caution and vigilance are required going forward
Friday – immense wealth is coming your way
Saturday – ruh roh…bad luck
Sunday – good luck will follow you

Rose Petal Magic

You can use the colour of the rose petals to bring in some colour magic.

- Red roses bring energy, passion and a boost of fire element.
- Pink roses have a softer energy but definitely use the energy of abundance and home comforts.
- Yellow rose has a happy, positive, good luck vibe.
- White roses are a good 'blank canvas' that can be used for any type of magic but lend themselves to clearing debts and opening up opportunities.

If you want to save some rose petals to use at a later date, they are easy to dry. Carefully pull each petal from the flower or pick up clean dry ones that the flower has already shed. Lay them on kitchen paper towels and put in a warm dry place, they will take a couple of days to dry fully. Then pop them in a jar or box and keep them to use later.

Money Making Mint

You can work with mint in all kinds of formats:

Fresh mint leaves
Dried mint
Peppermint essential oil
Peppermint flavouring
Peppermint tea
Peppermint sweets
Minty toothpaste
Mint scented shower gel

All of these carry the magic of mint and can be used in money making magic.

- Keep a mint leaf in your purse to ensure money keeps coming in.
- Dab your money or purse with mint oil to bring fast cash.
- Add a few drops of mint oil or a mint herbal tea bag to a bucket of hot water and use it to wash your floors and surfaces to bring prosperity to your home.
- Sprinkle dried mint under your front door mat to bring money into your home.
- Grow mint in pots and place by your doorways to bring in abundance.
- Charge your mint shower gel, soap or toothpaste with prosperity before you use it.
- Each time you eat a peppermint visualise money coming to you.

Money Making Ingredients

All of these ingredients have strong magical associations with money, prosperity and abundance. Some of them lend themselves more to being added to recipes and dishes that you can eat, to bring about the money magic. Others can be put into a small fabric pouch, envelope or jam jar, charge with your intent and then put it on your altar, hall table, mantlepiece or by your front door – all with the idea of bringing prosperity magic your way.

- Almond – brings prosperity and the promise of treasure. Pop an almond into your pocket or handbag to bring money in. Keeping an almond in your pocket is also said to lead you to treasure.
- Cashew nut – brings prosperity and energy. In fact, most nuts come with a big punch of prosperity energy.
- Cheese – is sacred to the Greek god Apollo and symbolises everything coming together and a successful outcome.
- Chestnut – brings strength, success, prosperity, abundance and fertility. Pop a few chestnuts around the house to bring in abundance and prosperity.
- Chocolate – brings prosperity, positive energy and happiness. Eat chocolate or use cocoa powder to bring that money magic in.
- Cinnamon – brings success, power, focus and helps with changes. Tie a bundle of cinnamon sticks with ribbon and hang on your tree or over your doorway to bring success.
- Cloves – bring money, clarity and abundance. Pop a clove into your purse or wallet to attract abundance.
- Ginger – brings power, success and prosperity. Pop a dab of ginger essential oil (or even ginger beer) onto your purse or wallet to bring money your way.
- Maple syrup – brings money, attraction and positive energy. Add to your recipes or pour on your breakfast,

maple syrup is not only delicious but attracts money to you.

- Nutmeg – brings money and luck. Carry a whole nutmeg with you for good luck and to attract money to you.
- Orange – brings happiness and generosity, and we could all certainly use that. Make your own pomanders by studding oranges with cloves and tying them on the tree or around the house with ribbons.
- Pear – brings prosperity and luck. Eat fresh or poach in wine for a delicious prosperity treat.
- Pecan nut – brings prosperity, in fact that is its primary magical correspondence. It works full on for prosperity and abundance. Keep a pecan on your desk to ensure that you keep your job.
- Star anise – brings luck. Place a piece of star anise into the corner of each room in your house to bring good luck your way.

Nut Magic

Nuts in fact are excellent for prosperity and abundance magic, some of them in particular such as:

- Almond – full of magic, the almond brings love, prosperity, treasure, intuition, psychic powers and passion your way. Use a few drops of almond oil or almond essence in your floor wash, pop an almond in your pocket or purse to bring money in. Keep an almond with you to lead you to treasure of all sorts.
- Brazil nut – brilliant for prosperity and love magic, carry one with you to bring good luck and send money your way.
- Cashew nut – brilliant for prosperity and a boost of energy, eat to bring you energy and use in spell work to increase prosperity.

- Sweet chestnut – a fabulous nut to use for strength, success, prosperity, abundance and fertility of all kinds. Pop a few chestnuts around the house to bring in abundance and prosperity. Eat them for fertility, success and strength.
- Macadamia nut – this is a high end, luxury full of richness nut so it works really well for prosperity and abundance.
- Peanut – the humble peanut whether it is in the form of a nut or peanut butter is packed full of masculine energy, it is the body builder of the nut world and brings a huge punch of prosperity magic. Eat peanuts or peanut butter to increase the size of your wallet and bring abundance your way.
- Pecan nut – fabulous in a pecan pie with all that gooey sugary goodness, the pecan brings prosperity and abundance your way. In fact, the pecan only has one magical job and that is for prosperity. Keep a pecan on your desk or in your drawer at work to ensure you keep your job.

Magical Honey

Honey can be added to any spell or recipe to make life sweet because it brings about the magic of happiness, love, prosperity and healing. Honey corresponds with the elements of both water so it can keep money flowing in and also the element of earth which represents all things material, abundance of all kinds and of course, money.

Honey is sacred to many of the ancient gods and was often used as offerings, you can do the same, put a drop of honey outside as an offering to bring abundance your way.

- Add a drop of honey to incense blends to bring prosperity to you.

- Add an image, an ornament or bee shaped jewellery to your altar or home to bring abundance magic in.

Don't forget to charge your honey or bee images with the intent of prosperity and abundance to get the magic started.

Pumpkin Seed Magic

Pumpkins are not only used at Samhain to scare away the ghosts and ghouls. They actually bring a huge punch of prosperity magic. You can use the seeds from the pumpkins, so once you have scooped them out for carving save the seeds.

Toasted pumpkin seeds – These are not only delicious, but they can also be eaten with the intent of bringing money your way. Rinse your pumpkin seeds in cold water. Put a pan of water on the hob and bring it to the boil, add a large pinch of salt. Pop the seeds into the boiling water. Boil until the seeds are soft. Drain the seeds and pat dry. Put the seeds into a large bowl and drizzle with olive oil, sprinkle with salt and dried rosemary. Preheat your oven to 350F/200C. Spread the seeds onto a lined baking tray. Bake in the oven for 20-25 minutes. Allow to cool. As you eat the pumpkin seeds make a wish for money and prosperity to come your way.

Pumpkin seed divination – You only need a handful of seeds for this. Wash and dry your pumpkin seeds. Place them in a small pouch or bowl. Ask the question 'when will money come to me' or perhaps 'how do I increase my cash flow' then take a handful of the seeds and throw them onto a flat surface in front of you. Look at how the seeds have fallen. Do they make an image or shape that you can translate to give you an answer?

Pumpkin seed pictures – Draw an image that represents money to you on a sheet of cardboard. It could be a pound or dollar sign or maybe a lucky four-leaf clover. Take some glue and paste it onto the image, now place pumpkin seeds onto the glue. This works quite well if you create the image at the beginning of October, then place it somewhere you will see it each day. As you glance at the seed image visualise each seed transforming into money. On 31st October you can bury or burn the image.

Feed the birds – Birds love pumpkin seeds! By placing your seeds out for the birds, you are thanking the Universe and Mother Nature for all that they provide. It is a little bit of gratitude but also a way of 'paying it forward' to help keep you in the money.

Prosperity Cookies

Sometimes I have odd chocolates that need using up (on a rare occasion). I like to use them up in my cookie recipe. Adding in a little money magic as well of course.

It doesn't matter what type of chocolates they are. You could also use any leftover nuts and/or figs and dates. Just chop them into small pieces.

Chocolate is rich and decadent and represents wealth. Nuts, figs and dates are all packed full of prosperity and abundant energy. Add that to you making good use of leftovers and you have the perfect money drawing food magic.

Recipe

110g/4 oz margarine
100g/3 ½ oz sugar
100g/3 ½ oz brown sugar
1 teaspoon vanilla extract
125g/ 4 ½ oz plain flour
56g/2 oz cocoa powder
1 teaspoon bicarbonate soda
¼ teaspoon salt

1 tablespoon milk
100g/3 ½ oz chocolates, figs, nuts or dates, chopped

- Preheat your oven to 350F/180C/Gas 4.
- Line a baking sheet with baking parchment.
- Whist the margarine and both sugars together until light and fluffy. Add the vanilla.
- In a separate bowl mix together the flour, cocoa powder, bicarbonate soda and salt.
- Add the dry ingredients to the wet and mix together. It will be crumbly.
- Add the tablespoon of milk and bring together to form a dough.
- Mix in the chocolate, nuts, figs or dates.
- The mixture will be thick but should be sticky enough to roll into small balls. Pop these onto the prepared baking sheet.
- Bake for 10 minutes. The edges will be firm but the centre still soft. They will firm up as they cool.

Magical Beverages

Let's take a look at the prosperity packed ingredients that you can use to make your favourite hot drink and turn it into a money-making slurp.

Tea – your usual black tea whether it is in a tea bag, or loose leaves carries a big punch of prosperity energy boosted by the element of fire and ruled by the Sun.
Coffee – in the form of instant, percolated or filter, your coffee brings a big punch of fire and Mars fuelled energy.
Chocolate – if drinking hot chocolate is your thing, then you are in luck because chocolate, in its raw form of cacao beans was once used for currency it was that highly rated.

It brings positive energy along with the magic of money, abundance and wealth.

Add an extra money-making boost to your hot beverage by adding in some extra ingredients or creating an herbal blend. Charge your ingredients before you add them to your mug or teapot, hold your hand over them and say:

"Magical money making come to me
I charge this drink with abundance and prosperity"

- Apple – add a slice of apple to your hot drink or warm up apple juice or cider. Apples have long been a symbol of abundance.
- Cashew – use cashew or almond milk, nuts all bring the magic of prosperity particularly cashews.
- Chamomile – chamomile tea is very calming and soothing, but it can also help to bring money in, because having money in the bank certainly brings a kind of peace to your life!
- Clove – pop a couple of cloves into your beverage to spice up your life and your finances. Don't add too many as it can be very medicinal tasting. Cloves at one time were extremely expensive and they still carry that abundance energy with them.
- Ginger – add a slice of root ginger to your hot drink or a teaspoon of ginger syrup, not only will it bring a zing of fire energy, but it also attracts success and prosperity.
- Honey – a spoonful of honey makes any herbal tea taste better! Honey can make your life and your bank balance sweeter with its sticky money-making energy.
- Jasmine – jasmine is an ancient plant and brings with it the knowledge and wisdom of money management.

- Maple syrup – add a spoonful of maple syrup to your coffee to make life sweet and to bring in the law of attraction. Maple syrup is all about drawing in and attracting all the good things in life and that includes money.
- Mint – peppermint is all about prosperity and keeping that money rolling in for you. Add a few springs of mint to your usual cuppa or make a peppermint tea.
- Nettle – nettles make an earthy tasting tea, much improved with a spoonful of honey, but nettles bring the magic of attraction and drawing money to you.
- Nutmeg – a pinch of nutmeg in your coffee is delicious and brings a fiery punch of money-making energy along with heap loads of positive luck.
- Peanut – add a spoonful of peanut butter to your coffee or hot chocolate to make a delicious magical abundant money-making beverage.
- Rose – a few rose petals in your cuppa will bring a lovely positive energy that sweeps in with abundance and happy vibes.
- Sage – sage in your cup of tea brings wishes, abundance and success by the cup full.
- Star Anise – the spicy star anise brings a lovely scent to your drink along with all the luck you need to boost your bank balance.

Manifesting Tea Magic

We all know that blissful moment of putting our feet up at the end of a hard day and sipping a hot cup of soothing tea. Relaxing, calming and apparently the answer to every situation "have a cup of tea it will make you feel better". But tea can also be extremely magical especially if you create the blends yourself and tie them in with your magical intent.

I have a beautiful teapot that has a built-in infuser, but you can get small metal infusers for individual cups of tea, and these are brilliant for popping your tea blends into or just use a normal teapot and a strainer, you will want to use one of these methods otherwise you will be spitting bits of herb and spice out.

I think there is something very magical about the whole process of making tea, especially if you make a bit of an effort rather than just throwing a tea bag into a cup and filling it up, it can become a small ritual in itself.

Don't like tea? Then follow the same magical process with your usual cup of coffee or drinking chocolate.

As you boil the kettle or warm the milk take a moment to visualise your goal, see money coming in, debts cleared and prosperity coming your way.

As you put the tea bag, herbs or coffee into the mug say:

"Manifesting mug of magic
Make the money come my way"

As you pour the hot liquid on top, along with your visualization, say:

"Now to heat things up and make it hot
Prosperity and abundance will be my lot"

Then stir it all together, turning the spoon in a clockwise direction to bring positive energy in.

"Stir this manifesting mug magic about
Prosperity and abundance find a route"

As you sip your drink, keep working with the visualization of prosperity and abundance. Once you finish, maybe leave a few dregs in the bottom of the cup and pour them out onto your garden as an offering to Mother Earth for what she provides for you.

Jam Jar Magic

Once you have finished your jar of jam or honey or even spice and herbs, what do you do with the empty jar? They can very easily be utilised for magic, money magic in particular.

Give it a good wash and dry and then set your intention to raise some cash with it. Set the jar by your front door and pop your spare change in it each time you come in; just the small coins will do. Not only will it actually add up to something useful when it is full it also brings positive money energy into the house.

Keep a clean empty jar and each day add a pinch of seeds to it, something like cumin or sesame seeds work well. Small seeds all represent prosperity, they might be small in size, but they are large in numbers. Filling up the jar with seeds is representative of filling up your bank account.

Another idea is to use uncooked rice grains. Rice is thrown at weddings to represent prosperity and fertility, so it works beautifully in money magic spells. Add a layer of rice then drop in a penny coin, sprinkle more rice over and add in a two pence coin, cover again with more rice and pop in a five pence coin. Fill to the top with more rice. I keep a jar like this on my hall table to bring money magic into the house.

Money Bowl

Such a simple idea that can be kept on your altar, beside your front door or on a window sill. Use a decent size bowl, a cereal bowl would work but a small fruit bowl is even better. Fill it with uncooked rice then add in your chosen items or ingredients. You can add a pinch of success with cinnamon and money bringing herbs such as basil or mint. Then put in items that represent money, it might be an old credit or bank card, silver or gold-coloured coins. Buttons and keys work well with the idea of opening up and unlocking new avenues of prosperity.

To kick the magic into action, stir the contents clockwise whilst visualising money coming in. Leave the bowl to do its thing but if you feel the need to recharge it or require some money fast give it another stir and make your request. You can boost the energy by adding in fresh items or ingredients.

When you feel it has done the work take out the coins, keys etc which can be cleansed and used again. Tip the rice and herbs into the trash and you can start again with fresh ingredients.

Money Powder

This powder blend is super easy to make and can be used in all kinds of situations.

- Put a pinch of money powder into your purse or wallet.
- Put a pinch of money powder into your handbag.
- Sprinkle the powder around the boundaries of your property to bring money in.
- Sprinkle some powder in each corner of your business property.
- Put a pinch of money powder into your shop till.
- Rub some powder on your money before you put it in your purse or wallet.
- Rub some money powder on your lottery ticket.
- Add a dab of money powder on your bills when they come in.

- Pop some money powder into a small pouch with a silver coin to carry with you.

The uses are endless. Create your mixture from 3, 5 or 7 of the following ingredients. Use your intuition about what to add but each of these ingredients carries prosperity and wealth and the ability to draw money to you.

Once you have selected which ingredients to use mix them together and if necessary, crush them in a pestle and mortar (or use the end of a rolling pin in a dish). Keep the mixture in a labelled jar.

Choose from:

- Dried basil
- Dried chamomile (you can use the contents of a chamomile tea bag)
- Ground cinnamon
- Cloves
- Coriander (seeds or ground)
- Cumin (seeds or ground)
- Ground ginger
- Dried mint
- Ground nutmeg
- Oats
- Poppy seeds
- Dried sage
- Sesame seeds
- Black tea (you can use the contents of a tea bag)

Fast Luck Oils

You can work with essential oil blends to bring money to you. Dab some of the oil on paper money to bring it back to you or pop a drop of oil in your purse to keep money coming in. Don't put essential oil straight onto your skin, some of them can cause irritation. If you want to use the oil to dab on your pulse points mix the essential oil blend with a base oil.

Fast Luck Oil – Use a few drops of each mixed together or pick out two or three that appeal to you.

Essential oils:

Cinnamon (use the oil but you can also add a piece of cinnamon stick to the mixture too)
Vanilla
Wintergreen
Mint
Lemongrass

Fast luck oil is often coloured red so you can add a drop of food colouring. The most commonly used ingredients for Fast Luck Oil are vanilla, wintergreen and cinnamon but I have also seen recipes that include mint and lemongrass too, but cinnamon is always the base used.

Money Draw Oil – Use a few drops of each mixed together or pick out two or three that appeal to you.

Essential oils:

Frankincense
Sandalwood
Myrrh
Cedar

Pyrite chips are often added to money draw oil.

Prosperity and Abundance Incense Blends

You can use incense sticks or cones to bring about prosperity and abundance energy but if you want to have a go at making your own money drawing loose incense blend it is easy. You will need to put this on a lighted charcoal disc to burn, bear in mind that using resin makes a lot of smoke. You can use most dried herbs, woods, spices and resins to create incense, just check to make sure they don't produce toxic smoke of course! I like to use equal quantities of each ingredient, but experiment and see what works for you. If you want to boost the scent add a few drops of corresponding essential oil.

Money Draw Incense

Pine resin
Cloves
Nutmeg
Mint

Abundance Incense

Frankincense
Rose
Clove
Patchouli

Let It Go

This magic will help you release and let go of those debts and the bad habits or cycles that allow us to get into debt in the first place. All you need to do is let it go...

Herbs and ingredients that can help you with releasing magic:

- Bay – bay purifies and cleanses along with bringing in some protection too.
- Carnation – carnation soaks up negative energy and helps bring about release.
- Chamomile – chamomile has a gentle cleansing and purifying energy that also helps draw money in.
- Cinnamon – cinnamon brings the magical energy to help you deal with changes and transitions.
- Coriander – coriander helps you to release the past and move forward.
- Fennel – fennel brings a cleansing, clearing and purifying magic to help you release.
- Ginger – the zingy energy of ginger can boost any magic.
- Lemon – the acid of lemon is purifying and can also help with decision making.
- Lime – lime works in a similar way to lemon bringing purification and cleansing it also gives a boost of energy to any spell working.
- Mint – mint cleanses and helps release negative energy and also brings a boost of prosperity magic.
- Orange – good for purifying and releasing but also brings an uplifting blast of solar energy.
- Parsley – parsley cleanses and releases along with an uplifting energy.
- Pine – pine purifies and helps release along with a punch of abundance energy.
- Rosemary – rosemary cleanses and purifies along with getting rid of anything that is unwanted!
- Sage – traditionally used to clear out unwanted and negative energy sage also helps bring in abundance and success.
- Salt – clears, cleanses and purifies along with bringing in protection.
- Star Anise – star anise brings a strong scent that clears and purifies.

- Thyme – thyme will bring in a purifying and cleansing energy that will help support you as you release and let go.
- Turmeric – turmeric brings about purification.

Prosperity Animals

These animals all have the magical energy and power to help you bring money in and boost your bank balance. It might be that you see one somewhere, even an image on a t shirt or piece of jewellery could be a sign. Or you can call in their energy to help you. Print out an image or photograph of one and keep it in your bag or purse to bring that wealth and prosperity energy in.

Bee – Without these little critters whizzing about in their stripy pyjamas we would have no food...they are incredibly important. Bees remind us to take the good stuff from life and to literally make hay (or honey) while the sun shines. Bee tells us to follow our dreams, but also with a reminder to plan and save for the future too. They represent prosperity, goals, achieving your dreams and good fortune.

Chicken – Chicken is all about fertility with a bit of sacrifice thrown in for good measure. The fertility comes from their egg-laying ability and the sacrifice bit from...well...being a sacrificial animal of choice throughout history. She does bring with her the essence of motherhood, nurturing, domestic bliss, being broody and fussing about. Chicken is in tune with the earth and herald's prosperity, rebirth and renewal along with abundance and comfort.

Horse – The horse seems to have devoted a huge part of its existence to serving mankind (thank you horseys). It works hard, carries, transports and is a companion – even the power of our cars is still measured in 'horsepower'. The horseshoe can be seen on many buildings, hung as a symbol of prosperity and good luck. There are several horse symbols carved into hillsides across the UK, all of which are associated with fertility. Definitely an animal of fertility of all kinds, including money and prosperity.

Unicorn – A mythical creature (or not...) stories about the unicorn can be found throughout the world. Usually, the unicorn is depicted as pure white with a long spiral horn (the allicorn) on its forehead, but it has been described as being many other colours. Unicorn is pure and innocent, which is why children will often connect very well with this animal spirit guide. They are said to be so fast that no one can ever catch one if they chase it, but if it comes to you, it can bring transformation, prosperity, strength, success, spirituality, changes, and valour. You possibly won't see one of these walking down the high street but there are plenty of images of them in all kinds of areas.

Rat – Such a misunderstood creature and blamed incorrectly for so many things. In some cultures, the rat is considered to bring fertility and wealth. Rats are definitely cunning and resilient creatures and although they do like to forage in the rubbish bins, they are actually very clean animals. Did you know that rats actually share their food with each other too? And they help each other out. They bring a powerful punch of energy for fertility, wealth, sharing and resourcefulness.

Grasshopper – The grasshopper sings with its body parts (but apparently generally only the males) and can leap over huge obstacles or into other dimensions, now that's something not everyone can claim to do. Grasshopper brings good luck and abundance, but also offers up opportunities for you to just leap right into, asking you to trust and not always to look before you leap. Jump forwards...never back.

Hedgehog – Definitely an earth element creature, the hedgehog brings a huge pack of earth magic along with abundance and fertility.

Mouse – Mice are um...let's just say they are prolific... so they represent not only fertility, but abundance too. They are also industrious, ingenious and good hoarders, conserving their resources.

Squirrel – Squirrel is a puzzle solver, there are not many obstacles that the squirrel can't work his way out of or over and he does so with complete perseverance. He is also a hoarder, packing away food to sustain him over the winter months; this guy is totally prepared, but he only takes what he needs. These things are good guidelines for us to follow.

Moon Magic

The moon carries enormous power. Any planet that can affect the tides of the world's oceans must be a force to reckon with. Add energy to your spells by working magic in the relevant moon phase.

Probably the most basic spell is to talk to the moon. Turn your face to hers and share with her your hopes and desires. She is always listening. Each moon phase lasts for about twenty-eight days. Starting with the dark sky, then a slither of the new moon that gradually increases (waxing) heading towards the full moon. Flowing onwards, the appearance of the moon slowly decreases back down (waning) to disappear completely, and the cycle begins again.

> New moon – Spells that focus on new beginnings, new projects and seeds of ideas. This phase also attracts abundance.

Waxing moon – This phase is all about bringing things to you and increasing them so that they gather momentum and grow.
Full moon – Excellent for divination of all kinds, seeking out opportunities and finding solutions to problems.
Waning moon – Reducing anything, clearing, cleansing and getting rid of bad habits, destructive cycles, removing obstacles and debt.

Sun Phases

Working with the phases of the sun throughout the day to increase your prosperity and reduce your debts. The sun has phases which can be used to tie in with your magical workings to add an extra boost of power. The sun measures time, where it sits in the sky denotes what time of the day it is, and a sun dial would be quite useless without the sun to cast a shadow! I also think that point between night and day and vice versa, that moment of hand over is quite special.

Sunrise – Basically when the sun wakes up and peers over the horizon. This phase is all about new beginnings, changes, employment, renewal, resurrection and finding the right direction. It can also be very cleansing. This is a good phase to start thinking about how to sort and increase your finances.
Morning – This is when the sun is growing in strength, so it brings the magical power for growth for your finances, positive energy, resolutions, building projects and plans, prosperity and expansion of ideas.
High noon – When the sun reaches its peak in the sky at midday – work magic for abundance, wisdom and knowledge.

Afternoon – The sun is heading back down, and the energy now is good for working on business matters, communication, clarity, travel, exploring and anything professional. Also, good phase to think about releasing some of those debts.
Sunset – As the sun takes itself off down below the horizon, work magic for removing debt, depression, stress and confusion, letting go, releasing or finding out the truth of a situation.

Think about your intention, whether it is to increase your savings, boost your income, find a better paying job or to decrease or remove your debts then work magic on the corresponding sun phase. A simple spell can be worked such as writing down your wish on a slip of paper and burning it, throwing it in the ocean or ripping it up (particularly good for getting rid of debts).

Prosperity Folklore

Here are some folk lore beliefs associated with prosperity and abundance. Keep them in mind and work with them, they will bring wealth your way.

- An old Chinese proverb says, 'a purse on the floor is money out of the door'. The belief being that you keep your precious items such as your purse, cards and money in your bag. To put the bag on the floor shows disrespect and shows that you aren't interested in your money. Keep that handbag off the floor!
- I was always told that being pooped on by a bird was lucky. Folklore upholds that belief. If it happens to you take it as a sign that prosperity is on the way, maybe even purchase a lottery ticket that day.
- If you happen to discover a tiny spider in your hair it is a sign of luck and abundance. Finding a spider and putting

it in your pocket will bring you wealth. I think the latter idea is a bit mean for the spider. If I find a spider on me, I thank it for its good luck and put it safely outside.

- A more modern belief is to keep the toilet lid shut when not in use. It helps prevent abundance from being flushed away.
- Placing the number 8 into the design of your home décor is believed to bring good fortune.
- Welcome a new baby into the family by gifting the child a silver coin, it will ensure they always have money in the future.
- Placing a silver coin in the shoe for a new bride will also ensure riches in the marriage.
- Feeling an itch in the palm of your hand? If it is the right hand then you will receive money, if it is the left hand then you will spend money.
- If you drop money onto the floor, put your foot on it first before you pick it up and say 'Money on the floor, money at the door' to ensure more cash comes your way.
- Most of us have heard the phrase 'find a penny pick it up, all day long you'll have good luck'. If you do see a coin out in the street check it first before picking it up. If the coin is heads up then it isn't lucky, turn the coin over so that it lies tails up and leave it for the next person. If you find the coin tails up, pick it up and take it with you for luck.
- If you gift someone with a new purse, make sure you put a coin in it. Giving an empty purse is bad luck; by adding a coin you will ensure the person always has cash coming in.
- Always cut your fingernails on a Friday, this will ensure financial success.

Spell Book

In this section you will find a selection of prosperity, abundance and debt releasing spells. Some of them are seasonal but all of them can be adapted to suit you and your needs.

Releasing Debt Spell Pouch

You will need:

An envelope
Three or four of the ingredients from the list above
Pen
Cauldron or fireproof dish
Matches or lighter

Take the envelope and write on the front

"I release myself from debt"

Now take the ingredients you have chosen. Take a pinch from the first one and add it into the envelope, saying:

"Magic of the herbal kind
Clear my debt leave nothing behind"

Take a pinch from the second ingredient, add it to the envelope and repeat the chant. Do this with each of your chosen ingredients.

Now seal the envelope and say:

"Sealing the deal, the debt will be gone"

Finally take the envelope and set fire to it, dropping it into the cauldron or fireproof container to burn out. Sprinkle the ashes to the wind, on your garden or into the trash.

Clean Up Your Finances!

This magic utilizes the magic within your cleaning products. Not only do you clean the house from a practical level you also clear your debts and tidy up your finances at the same time.

You will need:

Mop/cloth
Bucket/sink
Hot water
Peppermint, fennel or chamomile herbal tea bag

Fill your bucket or the sink with hot water, you can add a dash of your regular cleaning fluid if you wish. Now take the herbal tea bag in your hands and visualise your debts being cleared, and any money worries being washed away. Say:

"Power of herbals, magic to cleanse and free
Release my debt and make it clear to see"

Drop the tea bag into the hot water.

Now take your mop and clean your floors and using a cloth wash down all the windowsills and door frames. As you clean around, visualise your debts being washed away and cleared. You can repeat the chant as you work to add extra power.

Once you are finished, when you tip the dirty water down the drain, continue with the visualization of your debts being released with the water.

House Cleansing and Blessing Spell

What you will need:

Vacuum cleaner or broom
1 teaspoon dried basil (to bring in the money)
1 teaspoon dried mint (for abundance)
10 tablespoons of bicarbonate soda

Pop the bicarbonate of soda into a dish. Hold the dried basil in your left hand and visualise cleansing and clearing of negative energy from your home to allow new money sources to come in then drop it into the bicarbonate of soda. Next hold the dried mint in your right hand and visualise positive and abundant energy filling every room in your house. Drop the mint into the bicarbonate of soda and mix together.

Starting at the top of your home, sprinkle a small amount of the mixture on your floors in each room, working your way down and through each room in your house.

As you go you might like to chant:

"Basil to clear away the old and make way for the new
Stagnant energy is released for money to arrive that's due
Add in magical mint to the stash
Abundant and positive energy along with the cash"

Leave the mixture on the floors overnight, if possible, but for at least an hour, then vacuum the carpets or sweep the floors to clear up. You might like to repeat the chant as you vacuum.

Burn Your Debts Spell

This spell works even better if you work it on the waning moon, after the full moon when it is starting to disappear again. The waning moon brings banishing energy, so it adds to the power of the spell.

What you need:

A small black or white candle
Pen
Copy of your credit card bill or a piece of paper

Pin or a needle
Fireproof dish

- Take your credit card bill and circle the outstanding amount with the pen and then put a cross through it. If you don't have a credit card bill, write down your debts on a piece of paper and then put a big cross through the total owed.
- Fold up the bill, making the folds away from you as you want to get rid of the debt. The folding action helps add banishing energy if you fold it away from yourself.
- Using the pin or needle carve the figure you owe into the side of the candle.
- Place the candle on a safe surface.
- Light the candle and sit quietly for a few minutes visualising your debts vanishing and being replaced with sufficient funds.
- Then snuff out the candle. Place the folded bill under the candle and leave in a safe place.
- The next day set the candle safely and light it again. Sit for a few minutes and visualise your debts vanishing and money coming in.
- Snuff the candle again. Do this each day until the candle is burnt down.
- On the last day, after your visualisation take the folded bill and light it from the candle flame, dropping it safely into the fireproof dish and allow it to burn.
- Now throw the ashes away in the trash or flush them down the toilet, you want to get rid of them.

Now let the magic work. Remember that the cash probably won't just land in your lap, life isn't quite that easy, but you will see opportunities come your way to earn more cash or you might get a bonus at work. You may even receive money from an unexpected source. Trust.

Release Your Debt Spell

This spell can help clear your debts, but obviously you need to do the practical part yourself, sadly very rarely does a huge sum of money drop into our laps! The power of this spell will allow outside factors come in to help clear your debts. It might be a new source of income, the opportunity to sell some items you don't want or need, and you never know there is always the outside chance that you will win the lottery.

You will need:

A credit card or overdraft bill. If you don't have a printed-out copy, then you can use a blank sheet of paper.
An envelope that your credit card bill or any kind of bill came in, if you don't have one then use a plain new envelope.
A few pine needles
Pinch of dried mint
Pinch of salt
Pinch of ground ginger
A black candle in a safe holder
A white candle in a safe holder
Matches or lighter
Pen
Cauldron or fireproof dish

Set all your items out in front of you.
Light the black candle and say:

"Bringing light to the dark to clear and banish
This magic worked my debts will vanish"

Take your credit or overdraft bill and draw crosses over the balance owed. Make them big and bold and really obliterate the numbers with your pen. If you are using a blank sheet of paper, you can write the amounts you owe and who you owe them to in a list down the page.

Now write at the top of the paper "I release and banish all my debts", then turn the paper anti clockwise (to the left) and write the same sentence along the edge of the paper. Turn it again anti clockwise and write the sentence again along the edge. Do a final turn and write the sentence again. You should now have the same sentence written along all four edges of the paper.

Next take your ingredients and add a pinch of each to the centre of the paper. If you don't have one of the items don't worry, just add double of one of the other ingredients. Say:

"Power of pine needles, my debts go free
Cleansing energy of mint, release debt from me
Salt bringing the power of debts to banish
And ginger magic to make what I owe vanish"

Now fold the paper, taking the front piece and folding it over the ingredients, folding the paper away from you, then bring the sides and the top in so the herbs are all contained.

Slide your package carefully into the envelope.

Next write on the outside of the envelope – DEBTS BE GONE

Carefully hold the envelope over the candle flame so that you catch the edge of it alight.

Drop the burning envelope safely into the cauldron or fireproof dish.

Now light the white candle. Say:

"Bringing light to the dark, my debts are now banished
This magic worked today; my debts will now vanish"

Sit quietly and watch the flame. Visualise money coming your way and you being able to clear all your debts.

Allow both candles to burn out safely.
The ashes can be thrown in the trash.

Bucket and Spade Money Magic

Oh, I do like to be beside the seaside...bucket and spade in hand you can do some creative sand magic to increase your finances or to bury those debts for good.

To increase your finances, you might like to get busy and build a sandcastle. All those millions of grains of sand represent complete and unending prosperity. Build castles and visualise each one adding to money to your bank account. Add in decorative shells and pebbles to add more magic. Visualise as you go.

Build your prosperity sand castles as far away from the waves as you can, the further away, the longer the abundance magic will last.

To remove your debts, you need to put that spade to work! Collect some shells and/or pebbles from the beach. Then set about digging a hole in the sand. Make it nice and deep. When the hole is ready take each pebble or shell and drop it into the bottom of the hole. As you drop each one, say out loud "debt and money issues be gone". Drop as many pebbles or shells into the holes as you need to. Then start shovelling sand on top to fill the hole up. Once you are done say "my debts are now buried and gone, bad finances are done". If you feel inspired to, you might like to jump on top of the sand or even do a little dance...

Obviously, this magic needs some mundane back up, remember to think about the sand each time you are thinking about being frivolous with money.

Footprint Money Spell

Your feet connect you to the earth and the element of earth is all about stability, finances and worldly goods. Walking is also a useful tool, not only to get you from place to place but it moves energy as you go, it can carry that magic and make it work for you. Using your feet to carry magic that brings prosperity and money your way.

Here are some suggestions:

- Pop a basil or mint leaf (both herbs being excellent for prosperity and abundance) inside your shoe.
- Make yourself a foot powder to dust the bottom of your feet or to sprinkle inside your shoes:

5 tablespoons arrowroot or cornflour
2 tablespoons of baking soda
3 tablespoons dried herbs – a mixture of ground cinnamon, mint and basil, ground finely
Mix together and keep in an airtight jar.

- Draw a pound sign inside the bottom of each of your shoes, sandals of flip flops.
- Paint your toenails in a colour associated with money such as green, gold or orange. Paint one of your toes with a pound or dollar sign.
- Soil and sand both represent material things, take your shoes off and bury your toes in the earth of your garden or the sand on the beach and draw up the prosperity energy. Visualise that energy entering your feet. Then take nine steps, visualise money coming your way with each step. At the end of the ninth step say out loud 'make it so'. (Nine is a magical number, being three times three).

Harvest Sweeping

The broom or besom is a traditional symbol for sweeping out the old and bringing in the new. It is a feature of the hearth and home and all the good prosperity that it can bring. The act of sweeping is a natural gathering one.

You will need:

A broom, preferably a new one or make your own using a bundle of sticks tied together and fastened to a wooden pole.
Green ribbon (green is the colour for prosperity).
A small pouch
Dried mint
Dried basil
Dried grains – rice or barley work well

Take the pouch and add in the mint, saying:

"As the Wheel turns, and the first harvest is in
May this mint bring me money and prosperity within"

Then add the basil, saying:

"As the Wheel turns, and the first harvest is in
May this basil bring me money and prosperity within
And finally add the grains, saying:
As the Wheel turns, and the first harvest is in
May these grains bring me money and prosperity within"

Take the green ribbon and tie the pouch onto the handle of the broom.

Now go outside of your front door and hold the broom in both hands. Spend a few moments visualising harvesting what you desire; money, prosperity, bills paid, items required, whatever it might be. See it all clearly in your mind.

Take the broom and start sweeping towards your door. You don't need to actually touch the ground with the broom (you don't want lots of dirt and dust being swept into your house) this is symbolic so keep the bristles just above the floor. Say:

"As I sweep one, two, three
I sweep the harvest prosperity
As I sweep two, three, four
I bring abundance through my door"

Repeat this chant three times and then go back inside. If you have the space, keep the broom in the heart of your home and use it regularly when you need money coming in.

Debt Releasing Knot Spell

Tying knots into twine sets your intention, then the action of untying them or burning releases the magic. You can use this premise to record your debts and then let them go, sending magic out to the universe with a request to provide the money and/or ways of earning extra money to pay off what you owe. I suggest using a 33-inch piece of twine here because 13 is a magical number and allows you space to tie the number of knots needed.

You will need:

A piece of twine or ribbon 13 inches long (33cm) – it must be made from material that will burn safely
A white candle in a safe holder
Lighter or matches
Cauldron or fireproof dish

Place your candle in front of you and light the wick. Pick up your piece of twine and hold it in both hands saying:

"I work now with the magic of knots and string
To release my debts and money to bring"

Now start to tie your knots, space them out so that you have room to tie nine knots in total. Start with tying the first knot and say:

"By the knot of one my magic is begun"

Tie the second knot and say:

"By the knot of two, I know what I need to do"

Tie the third knot and say:

"By the knot of three, I release my debts from me"

Tie the fourth knot and say:

"By the knot of four, money opportunities arrive at the door"

Tie the fifth knot and say:

"By the knot of five, my prosperity thrives"

Tie the sixth knot and say:

"By the knot of six, my finances are fixed"

Tie the seventh knot and say:

"By the knot of seven, financial success is given"

Tie the eighth knot and say:

"By the knot of eight, my finances are great"

Tie the ninth knot and say:

"By the knot of nine, financial stability is mine"

Sit quietly with the knotted cord in your hands and watch the candle flame for a few moments, visualise money and opportunities coming to you and your debts being paid off.

Lastly light the end of the cord from the candle flame and allow it to burn, dropping it into the cauldron for safety. End the spell by saying:

"This cord spell is now at an end
Magical energy now to me lend"

Sweeping Spell

There is an old folk tradition that says on the first day of the new year open your back door and let out the old negative energy. Then open the front door to let in the new year fresh and positive energy. So, this spell works with that idea, although you can work it at any time of the year.

You will need:

Incense stick/cone or a scented candle (and holder)
Lighter/matches

Open the back door of your house and the windows. Starting at the top of your house. Light the incense or candle. Go into each room and walk anti clockwise around. (Anti clockwise removes negative energy). Waft the incense smoke or candle scent around the room and into each corner. As you do so, say:

"As the old fades away
Clear out the negative energy today"

Do this in each room, working your way around each room upstairs then moving downstairs. Ending up by your back door.

Stand at the doorway and say:

"Out with the old, the bad and the debt
So mote it be!"

Now close the back door and the windows then open the front door.

Starting from that point go into each room downstairs and walk clockwise (clockwise brings the positive energy in). Go around each room wafting the smoke or scent into each corner. Say:

"A new start, fresh for this year
Bring money and prosperity to me, right here"

Work your way through each room and then upstairs.

Once you have done every room leave the candle burning safely if you wish or snuff it out. Let the incense burn out. Finally say:

"Blessings of prosperity are welcome to this house
Make it so!"

Then close the front door.

Releasing Debt Spell

It can be very easy to fall into debt, it happens to a lot of us. Don't beat yourself up about it. But see if you can do something to let go of it and rebuild. This spell will help you release any debts you have (as in repay them quickly) and stop you from going down that particular rabbit hole again. It is all about breaking the cycle.

What you need:

A bill or credit card statement, something that shows your debt
A black or dark coloured candle and safe holder
Lighter or matches
Fireproof dish
Dried sage
Dried thyme

Set your black candle in front of you and light it. Take your debt paperwork and tear it up into small pieces. Visualise your debt being repaid and no longer having a hold over you. Take each piece of paper and light it from the candle flame and carefully drop it into the fireproof dish. After each piece add a pinch of sage and thyme into the fireproof dish. As you add the herbs say:

"Enough money will come my way
To allow me now my debts to pay
Letting go and releasing my debt
All monies owed by me will now be met"

Do this as many times as you need until all the pieces of paper have been burnt.

Snuff the candle out and dispose of the candle stub and the ashes in the dustbin.

Flame Those Debts

This spell uses the principle of burning that which we want to get rid of. Let's start with credit card bills and loans. Obviously, fire won't make it all suddenly disappear, but it will help move the energy so that other ways to pay off your debts will appear.

You will need:

A credit card bill or loan statement (more than one if you have them)
A red, orange or yellow candle in a safe holder
Lighter or matches
A fireproof dish or cauldron
A black marker pen

Place all your items on a safe surface in reach. Light your candle. Spread your credit card bill or statement in front of you. Take your black marker pen and draw a line through the amounts you owe on the statement and say:

"Clearing and cleansing energy of fire
Help rid my debt as is my desire"

As you cross out the figures visualise money coming in to enable you to pay off your debts. Now carefully take the candle and tip it so that a few drops of candle wax drip onto the credit card statement. Repeat the chant three times.

Place the candle safely back in the holder. Fold the statement starting with the bottom of the sheet, folding it away from you, then fold the top in and the sides. Folding the paper away from you helps remove energy. Now take the folded statement and catch the corner alight from the candle, drop it into the cauldron to burn. Repeat the chant three times more.

Visualise becoming debt free.

Snuff out the candle and dispose of the stub in the trash. Tip the ashes onto the garden or into the trash.

Dissolving Your Debts

Use the power of water to clear and wash away your debts, bills and loans. Obviously, it won't just magically make them disappear, but it could help to bring extra income or windfalls of money your way to help pay them off.

You will need:

Half a cup/mug of plain flour
Water in a jug
Bowl for mixing
Wooden spoon
Rolling pin
Large pinch ground cinnamon
Sharp knife
Dish or tray that can hold a couple of inches of water

Take the bowl for mixing and tip the flour into it. The amount doesn't need to be exact, just take your usual coffee mug and fill it about halfway with flour.

Hold your hand over the flour and say:

"Flour magic, prepare to absorb
Show my debts and bills the door"

Add in the pinch of ground cinnamon and say:

"Add in the energy of cinnamon for success"

Next pour a little of the water into the flour, just a small amount at a time. Mix with the wooden spoon. You want to add enough water to bring it together to form a dough, as if you were making pastry. Now roll out the dough on a flat surface, it doesn't need to be very big.

Then you write the amount of money you need to cover all your debts by scratching the figure into the dough with the tip of your sharp knife. Once that is done carefully lift the dough from the surface and place it on the bottom of your dish or tray.

Now pour water over the top of the dough. As you do so, visualise the water dissolving your debts and money you owe. Say:

"Power of water, cleansing and pure
Dissolve my debts, make them no more"

Once the dough is covered with water you can leave it to do its thing or you can get your hands in there and help it along, squish the dough between your fingers and allow it to melt into the water. As you do so, use your visualisation again to see your debts disappearing. The visualisation adds to the energy of the spell.

Once you are done you can leave the dish outside for the sun to evaporate the water, then tip the dough remains into the trash. Or drain the liquid off and throw the remnants away.

Cleansing and Clearing

There are numerous ways to clear away negative energy that can build up and cause bad luck or bad habits in spending. We can also work magic to cut ties to old negative ways and bad habits. Clearing out the old, negative cycles and bad patterns makes way for the good and positive ones to ride on it. Leaving them in place just allows them to fester and get worse.

Smudge your home to clear out negative energy:

You will need:

Incense – loose on charcoal or an incense cone or stick – choose a scent that works for you, but I like to use something fresh such as mint, lavender, patchouli or sandalwood.
Matches or a lighter
A safe holder for your incense

Light your incense and carry it around your home. Start at the front of the house downstairs and work your way to the back, then upstairs. Go into each room and waft the smoke around, make sure you waft it into all the corners too. Say:

"Negative energy now be gone
Bad habits, bad luck and hardship is done
Bring in the positive, make it pure
Prosperity and abundance now for sure"

Once you have done the whole house you can leave the incense to burn out safely. If you don't like working with smoke this can be done with salt water – add a pinch of salt to a bowl of water and give it a stir. Flick the water into the corners of each room. Alternatively use sound, bang a drum or clap your hands around your home, using the same chant.

It is surprising how quickly negative energy builds up; I like to work a smudging routine on a regular basis.

To boost the cleansing and keep the energy running you can also place crystals around your home that soak up negative energy and transform it into positive, bringing abundance and prosperity. Pop a crystal on a shelf or windowsill in the central room of your home. I would suggest crystals such as blue lace agate, fluorite, moonstone, clear quartz or rose quartz.

Cutting Ties to Bad Spending Habits

It can be easy to slip into bad spending habits and we have all done it. The difficult part is stopping that destructive cycle before it spirals out of control. Magic can help with the initial break, but you will need to put some work in yourself to follow up the spell.

You will need:

Scissors
A piece of twine, string or ribbon – approximately 1m long
Two sheets of paper
Pen or pencil
Candle in safe holder – black or white are good colours to use
Matches or a lighter
Cauldron or fireproof dish

Set all your items in front of you. Light the candle and say:

"Guiding light, bring clarity to me
Show my bad spending habits and set me free"

Now take a sheet of paper and write down your debts and your outgoings, be honest and also note what you have spent them on. This is particularly for those debts that have arisen from bad habits or frivolous spending. It could also be a good way of seeing where all your money is going, it can highlight some areas where changes can be made. Take your time with this.

Next take a second sheet of paper and write down your income and any areas where you can bring money in. Also add goals and desires for how you wish your finances to be, even if you just write the words 'debt free'. Take your time with this too.

Now roll up the first sheet of paper and tie it up with one end of the piece of twine. Roll up the second sheet of paper and tie it up with the other end of the piece of twine so they are joined with a length of twine in between each. Hold one roll in your left hand and the other in your right hand and say:

"Bad spending habits and wasted money is done
I release the negative energy so there is none
Set me free with the cutting of cord
Change my ways to work with what I can afford"

Place the rolls of paper on the surface in front of you and pick up the scissors, cut the twine in half. Repeat the chant as you cut.

Now take each roll of paper complete with the twine and light it from the candle, dropping it safely into the cauldron to burn. Say:

"Flame and fire bring me release
From debt and bad spending now give me peace"

Once they have burnt out you can sprinkle the ashes onto your garden or into the trash.

Release Those Debts!

We all spend too much money over the festive season, and it is easy to rack up debts so let's use the fresh new energy of January to release and let go some of them. For this spell we are using the fresh scents that herbs and spices bring and a bit of a fiery boost to make the transformation happen.

You will need:

A cauldron or fireproof dish
A candle left over from Christmas or a black or white one in a safe holder
Matches or a lighter
A piece of Christmas gift wrap or the front of a Christmas card
A pen
Pinch of fennel seeds
Pinch of mustard powder

Take your left-over Christmas candle and set it in a safe holder and place it in front of you, light the wick. Now say:

"Christmas candle, now the festive season is done
Help me work to make the holiday debt be gone"

Take a piece of Christmas gift wrap, the front of a Christmas card or a piece of paper if you don't have either. Set it in front of you and write on it:

Christmas spending is now at an end
Changes will now be made so I don't spend
Look to clear my festive debt now
All I ask is that you show me how

Take a pinch of fennel seeds and sprinkle them into the centre of the piece of paper and say:

"Fennel seeds sweep through and clear
All my festive debt without fear"

Take a pinch of mustard powder and sprinkle it into the centre of the piece of paper and say:

"Mustard powder fiery and hot
Boost the purpose of this spell a lot"

Now fold the paper over from the back to the centre, the front to the centre and then each side to form a little parcel. Carefully take the parcel and light the edge from the flame of the candle, drop it into the cauldron to burn out. Visualise your debts disappearing and say:

"Transformation power of flames and fire
Know that debt free is to what I aspire"

Snuff the candle out and snap the rest of the candle in half. Throw the candle pieces into the trash and tip the ashes of the burnt paper and herbs onto the soil or into the bin

A Prosperity Package

Once you have worked magic to clear your debts you might like to open some avenues to bring in new cash. This prosperity package puts all your wishes into a parcel, then using the power of flame and fire we send the intent out into the universe. All the contents of the parcel need to be easily burnt, without giving off toxic fumes.

You will need:

A large sheet of paper, I like to use brown paper, but any will do
A piece of natural twine (it will burn so don't use anything toxic)
A bonfire, fire pit, fireplace, chimenea or BBQ

Pinch chilli powder or chilli flakes
Pinch cocoa powder
Pinch ground cinnamon or piece of cinnamon stick
A handful of dry rice
Pinch of sugar
A felt tip pen or biro

Lay out your sheet of paper in front of you. Take your pen or biro and write across the paper

Fire magic bring to me
Money, prosperity and financial security

Now add in your 'ingredients', placing them in a pile in the centre of the sheet of paper. Start with the dry rice and say the chant, then add the pinch of sugar followed by the spices and chilli saying the chant again as you add each ingredient.

Once all your items are added end with the chant 'sugar and spice to make all things nice'.

Now fold the paper up to make a small parcel and tie it with the twine. Fold the paper from the top towards you first, then from the bottom and the sides. Folding the paper towards you brings the energy in.

Hold the parcel in both hands and visualise new pathways of money opening up to you with new projects and ventures.

Once your parcel is ready, throw it into the flames and let the fire work its magic.

Abundance Cheque Spell

Every new moon I work an abundance cheque spell. I have been doing this regularly for several years now and it has never let me down. Work on the new moon as this helps boost the magic of bringing positive energy and prosperity towards you.

You will need:

> A blank cheque – this can be from your own cheque book, but I prefer to download one from the internet, just do a search for "abundance cheque" and you will get lots of options and designs to print off.
> A pen – I like to use green as this is a colour associated with money
> A pinch of cocoa powder
> A pound coin

On your cheque in the space where it says 'pay to the order of' write your own name. Where it has space for the amount to be paid write 'paid in full' both in the figures box and the line for words. For the date write 'now'. Sign it 'The Universe'.

Sprinkle a pinch of cocoa powder into the centre of the cheque. Say:

> *"Abundance, power of cocoa, draw money to me*
> *I ask the Universe for prosperity I can see"*

Then fold the cheque, bringing the paper edge towards you, folding the paper a couple of times over. Folding the cheque towards you brings in the action of drawing money to you. Folding it away from you will send money out, don't do that! Once it is folded neatly, draw a £ sign on the top of the folded paper.

Hold it in both hands and visualise money coming to you and your bank account being full.

Then pop it in a safe place with the pound coin placed on top.

Keep it there for the whole month, then on the next new moon you can dispose of the cheque either by burning it or throwing it away as it will have worked its magic. Then you can write a new one for the coming month.

New Moon Prosperity Spell

You will need:

The new moon phase (most diaries have a note of this, but charts can be found online)
A white candle
Four green candles
A compass (or compass app on your phone)
A gold coin (£1 or £2)

Working this spell on the new moon will add attraction and new sources of prosperity energy to your magic.

- The white candle represents you and 'the all'.
- Green uses colour magic to represent prosperity and money.
- The compass is used to find the directions but also symbolises your direction in life.
- The coin does what is says…it represents money and prosperity.

Tip: Use birthday cake candles, they are cheap and easy to source. If you can't find or don't have green candles, then white ones are a good 'multi-purpose' choice.

We will be working with the four compass directions; North, South, East and West these all have meaning:

North – finances, stability and material matters
East – intellect and inspiration
South – passion and energy
West – Emotions, intuition and releasing

Place your white candle in the centre of a safe level space. Use your compass (or app) to ascertain the four directions of North,

South, East and West. Place a green candle at each of the four directions, in a square around the main white candle. Place the coin between the white candle and the green candle in the North. Light the white candle.

Say this chant or one of your own, three times out loud. At the end of each chant turn the coin over:

"Drawing magic from the new moon
Bring to me, fresh opportunities and new money soon
As I turn this gold coin around
Prosperity and financial security to me in abounds"

Then starting with the green candle in the North, light all four saying at each direction:

"New moon money arrive in from the North
New moon money blow in from the East
New moon money blast in from the South
New moon money wash in from the West"

Sit quietly watching the flames and visualise money flowing to you and doors opening for new opportunities. Finish by saying:

"make it so".

Extinguish the candles and pop the coin in your purse.

Prosperity Egg Spell

What you will need:

A pebble or small tumble stone crystal
An egg cup or small cup
A small bowl, slightly bigger than the egg cup

A second bowl, slightly larger than the other
A jug of water

If you work this spell on a Thursday, you will get an added abundance boost from the energy of Jupiter. Cast during a waxing moon phase to also ramp up the money vibe.

Set the largest bowl on a flat surface. Place the smaller bowl inside and then the egg cup inside that. Pop your pebble or crystal inside the egg cup. Pebbles carry the energy of the element of earth which is all about stability and material goodies. If you use a crystal, pick one that resonates with you, I like to use a green crystal for prosperity magic, but trust your intuition. Pour the water into the egg cup and keep pouring, allowing the water to overflow into the smaller bowl. Visualise money coming in to you and all your financial needs being met as you do so. You might like to chant, something like:

"Money, money come to me
Prosperity, abundance and financial security
Allow my cup to overflow
And my bank account, money to show
As is my will, make it so!"

Keep pouring until the water overflows into the largest bowl. Say a little thank you and use the water in your garden or for pot plants. Pop the crystal/pebble into your purse or bag.

Chicken and Egg Prosperity Spell

This spell draws upon the fertility energy of the egg and the prosperity and abundance energy of the chicken. If you have access to the internet and a printer you can print off an image of a chicken. If you have a chicken ornament or children's toy that could be used too.

You will need:

An egg in its shell
An image of a chicken
A green or yellow candle in a safe holder
Lighters or matches
Sharpie or felt tip pen

Set your items in front of you and look at the chicken image, focus on it and get the idea of chicken being prosperity and abundance set into your mind. Say:

"Energy of chicken I call to thee
Bring your prosperity magic to me
Chicken abundance and fertility
Now join this spell lend your help to me"

Light the candle. Sit quietly and focus on the candle flame, visualise money and prosperity coming your way.

Now carefully take the egg and the pen. Draw the pound or dollar symbol onto the shell of the egg or write the word 'money'. Keep writing money words and symbols onto the shell until you have covered it all. As you do this, say:

"Energy and magic from the chicken and eggshell
Draw prosperity and abundance to me and make it sell
Bring money now and make it quick
From working this egg and chicken trick"

Hold the egg in your hands and sit for a moment, still visualising money coming in and opportunities opening up for abundance to come your way.

When you are ready snuff out the candle. Take the egg and bury it beneath the soil in your garden. Or you could use a plant pot filled with soil. The egg will break down and feed the earth, whilst releasing your money magic request.

Egg Magic

This is an easy method of working some magic to make your savings grow or to bring money your way. It isn't a quick fix for cash, but it will work slowly and surely to bring financial stability.

Take a raw egg and carefully write with a felt tip pen around the shell. You could just write one word such as 'money' or 'prosperity' but if you have small handwriting you might want to put 'bring money to me' or 'increase my bank balance'. Then bury the egg in your garden. If you don't have a garden the egg can be buried in some soil in a plant pot. As the egg breaks down it will not only feed the soil and the plants it will also bring prosperity your way.

It works by using the symbolism of the egg as fertility but also bringing into play the four elements: earth for stability and material things, air for intellect and money wise ability, fire for energy and water for keeping emotions stable.

Money Map Spell

You may have heard of the term 'mind map'. This is a tool used to open up your thought process and get ideas from your head out into reality. I like to use this process to create a money map spell.

You will need:

A piece of paper
A pen or pencil
Pinch of ground cinnamon or dried basil (both represent money)

Sit quietly with the paper in front of you and write the word 'money' in the centre of the paper and draw a circle around it. Now let your mind drift and write any words that come to your mind when you think of money. What you need to spend it on and what you would like to spend it on if you had more. Write the words or draw images on the paper, anywhere on the sheet that you feel is right.

Take some time with this. Put the necessities on there as well as luxuries or treats.

When you are finished draw lines from the central money word to each of the other items.

Then sprinkle the cinnamon or basil on the centre and fold the paper up. Bringing the outer edges in until you have a little package. Hold it in your hands and say:

"Money map from my mind
Draw prosperity and cash to me
To leave debt and wanting behind
So mote it be!"

Bury the package in your garden or burn it safely.

Money Mind Map Magic

Whenever you are looking to create a new beginning or open up new opportunities, I find it helps to open my mind to see what ideas I can bring to the table. This mind map spell helps to focus those thoughts.

You will need:

A sheet of paper
A pen or pencil
A cauldron or fireproof dish
A white candle in a safe holder

Lighter or matches
Spoonful of uncooked rice
Spoonful of porridge oats

Set your candle in front of you and light the flame, as you do so say:

"Candlelight help guide my mind
Ideas for prosperity for me to find"

Place the sheet of paper in front of the candle and begin by writing the word 'money' in the centre of the paper. Now sit quietly and focus on the word 'money' then begin to jot down any other words that come into your head. Write them randomly on the paper, wherever you feel they need to be, spread them out and use the whole sheet of paper. It doesn't matter what the words are or how silly they might seem, write them on the paper.

When you are done sit back and take a look at the words. See if any of them spark an idea or jolt your brain into action with new plans or ideas for money making. Don't worry if they don't, just read through all of the words, the idea might come to you later.

Now take the rice and sprinkle it into the centre of the paper and say:

"Fertility of new ideas from rice
Make my life financially nice"

Then take the oats and sprinkle them into the centre of the paper and say:

"Oats bring new money to me
Allow me to wallow in prosperity"

Carefully fold the paper, bringing the top half over to the middle, the bottom up to the centre and then fold the sides in to make a little parcel.

Take the parcel and light the corner of it from the flame of the candle, then drop it into the cauldron and say:

"Money making magic set into a mind map
Prosperity and abundance is now a wrap!"

Allow it to burn out and sprinkle the ashes onto the ground. Let the candle burn out and dispose of the stub in the trash.

Money Flow Spell

Work this spell on a full moon for extra power. You will only need the money you have in your purse or wallet, no matter how little that might be. This spell needs to be worked outside to help the energy flow and not be restricted by the walls of your home.

Lay the coins and notes you have in front of you and one by one turn them over. Repeat this chant:

"By the power of the full moon
Allow the flow of money to me soon
Let prosperity find its way
Money rain upon me from this day"

Then you can put the money back into your purse. If you want to add a little bit of magical herb boost you can also dab the money with peppermint oil or sprinkle some dried mint over it.

Opportunities Jar

In January I like to have a good clear out, physically, mentally and spiritually. I clear my altar completely and just lay a white cloth on it. I don't place anything back onto the altar for a few days, and then only one piece at a time. I like to use the energy of January to leave space for new opportunities to come my way. Leaving the space on my altar is representative of that. You can also work a jar spell to do the same thing. You could work this spell at the beginning of any month, it doesn't need to be January.

You will need:

A clean empty jam or pickle jar.
Sharpies, pens, paint or stickers.
Incense or a scented candle
Matches or lighter

Place the items in front of you. Light the incense or scented candle then take the jar and hold it upside down over the smoke or flame. Visualise this filling the jar and cleansing it, clearing out any negative energy. Say:

"January brings a new year
A clear out of negative energy and fear
Cleansing, clearing, out with the old
Ready and willing for the new and the bold"

Once you feel the jar is clear turn it right side up. Now take your pens, paint or stickers and create a design on the outside of the jar. You are aiming to create something that says you are open to opportunity, new ventures, new business and all the prosperity and abundance you can get to come your way. You might like to draw pound or dollar signs, maybe lucky four-leaf clovers or just a design that makes sense to you. Visualise new opportunities opening up and money coming your way as you do your design. Don't forget to add your design to the lid of the jar too.

When you are done hold the jar in front of you and say:

> *"Empty space is open and ready*
> *Abundance and opportunity flow nice and steady"*

Now put the lid on the jar and say:

> *"This is now my opportunity and abundance jar*
> *May it fill with good things from wide and far"*

Place the jar near your front door to bring in positive energy or place it on your altar.

Honey Jar Spell

This spell works with the prosperity magic of honey to help you sweeten your bank account and make money stick. If you have an empty honey jar with the last dregs of honey in, this works perfectly – don't wash it, just use it as it is.

You will need:

A jar with a lid
Honey
Slip of paper
Pen
A small candle (green, gold or yellow)
Matches or a lighter

If you are not using a honey jar with the dregs in, you will need to add a spoonful of honey to the bottom of the jar. Then take the slip of paper and write the words in the centre:

Honey makes money

Fold the slip of paper towards you and then drop it into the jar.

Say three times:

"Sticky and sweet the abundance of honey
Bring cash to me and make lots of money"

Now add a spoonful of honey on top of the paper in the jar. And repeat the chant three more times. Put the lid on the jar. Hold the candle and light the wick, carefully drip some of the wax onto the lid and then quickly set the candle on top so the wax helps it stick to the lid. Allow the candle to burn out, whilst visualizing money coming to you and life being sweet with abundance.

When the candle has burnt out the jar can be put into the trash.

Prosperity Herb & Flower Jar

Use this jar of magical herbs and flowers to increase your prosperity and bring money into your home. Add a variety of dried plant matter to a clean jar, give the jar a gentle shake then inhale the scent before you do any of your finances, go shopping or step out of the house. You can even pop some of the mixture into a small pouch (the organza wedding favour ones are good for this) or into an envelope and pop it into your handbag. When you are out shopping and want to curb your spending take a sniff from the pouch. Or if you want to pick your lottery numbers do the same.

You can add whatever herbs, flowers and spices resonate with you for prosperity purposes but some good ones to use are basil, honeysuckle, rose, bergamot, chamomile, clover, goldenrod, honesty, jasmine, mint, dill, nutmeg, cloves, oak leaves, ginger and poppy.

You don't need to use all of these just whichever ones feel right for you or add your own choices. To keep it simple you can also just use one type of herb, flower or spice.

As you add the plant matter to the jar you might like to say a few magical words, such as:

"Mother Nature bring your power
Beauty of the plants underneath a bower
Flowers, herbs and spices go
Into my prosperity jar to make money flow
Deeply inhale, the wonderful scent
Money and prosperity are now meant"

If you prefer you can keep a vase of fresh flowers beside your door. Just before you leave to go out, smell the flowers and remind yourself of the prosperity magical chant.

Balance Your Finances Spell

This simple spell will help you balance your finances using simple natural items.

You will need:

A shell
A pebble
An elastic band or piece of string
Marker pen

The shell represents the element of water, this is the part of us that makes impulse buys based on our emotions and feelings. I bet we have all done that at some point! The pebble is for the element of earth, this covers finances, prosperity, grounding and stability. The element of earth puts our feet firmly back on the ground and brings a stability to our spending. Earth is also strongly associated with prosperity and the material things in life.

Using the pen draw a £ sign on the shell. Then draw another £ sign on the pebble. Hold one in each hand. Sit quietly and visualise yourself making sensible purchases. See your bank account nice and healthy and your savings account too. Paint a picture inside your head of you and your family being financially stable. Paying back loans and receiving extra money. It's your visualisation, let it take you where it needs to go.

When you are ready place the shell and the pebble together with the £ signs facing each other. Now wrap the elastic band or string around them both. Tying them together securely. The bonding of them together shows the universe that you are committed to being financially sensible and that you are worthy of receiving.

As you bind them together say:

"Element of water, bring my emotions and spending habits into check
Element of earth, stability and security are now at my call and beck
The binding is now secure, let the magic flow
Make it so!"

Place the shell and pebble where it can be seen regularly, on a bedside table or on a mantelpiece – this will remind you of the magic you have worked, and the commitment made.

Fast Money Magic Pouch

Medicine bags, magic pouches, gris gris or mojo bags are fabulous to work with. (All different names for pretty much the same thing). A magic pouch contains items that are charged with your intent and each item is a guide for the spirits to help them understand what the outcome you desire is. A magic pouch can contain all sorts of items – herbs, roots, spices, crystals, feathers, bones, shells, dirt, pebbles, coins - what you put in your medicine bag is up to you.

I like to add colour magic to my magic pouches, I use orange material a lot as this is the colour for success, but also using green for prosperity. You don't even have to be good at sewing, just use a handkerchief or felt is good as that doesn't need hemming, or just use a scrap of material. They can be tied with string or ribbon. You can also use the organza bags that craft shops sell for wedding favours. Be creative.

You will need:

A green pouch with a drawstring or a piece of green fabric and ribbon

A feather – this brings the element of air which helps things to move quickly.

A whole nutmeg – nutmegs are associated with luck and prosperity.

6 silver coins, 5p coins work perfectly for this. As coins they represent prosperity but the addition of being silver also boosts the money magic.

A pinch of dried basil – an herb that helps bring money your way.

A pinch of dried mint – an herb that boost prosperity.

A pinch of cinnamon – this spice is not only all about success it also gives a fiery boost of energy to the whole spell.

Hold each item/ingredient in your hand and visualise money pouring into your hands/purse/bank account really quickly. Say:

"Money, money come to me
With speed and agility
Money, money right now to me
Fast abundance and prosperity"

Then drop the item into the pouch. When all the items are in tie the bag tie the top firmly and say the chant again, three times.

I like to leave the pouch outside in the sun for an hour or so, particularly at noon when the sun is at its height – it helps to charge the spell with positive sunshine energy. Then pop the pouch into your bag.

A Fruitful Spell

This spell work well at the height of summer, fresh fruit is in season, plentiful and inexpensive. This is an edible spell (my favourite kind) and can involve the whole family or friends.

What you will need:

A variety of fresh fruit to make a fruit salad such as:
Melon
Pineapple
Strawberries
Blueberries
Grapes
Oranges
Apples

As you start to clean and chop the fruit, focus on each type as you do so, adding it to a large bowl.

- So, as you chop the melon think about cutting up your money worries, visualise them disappearing.

- Then with the pineapple, as you add the chunks to the bowl visualise each one being money that you add to your bank account.
- For the strawberries, each one could be loose change that you find.
- Grapes are good for abundance so as you add them to the bowl see them bringing abundance to you.
- Blueberries are excellent for protection so add them to the bowl with the intent of protecting your spell.
- Apples are also good for abundance so as you chop them and add them to the bowl visualise a healthy bank balance.
- Oranges are good for luck and money so focus on this as you add them to the bowl.

When you are done as you serve each person give them a blessing of abundance and prosperity. You could even have your guests say 'make it so' as a blessing of thanks.

Prosperity Candle Spell

What you need:

A green, gold or brown candle – use a small candle so that it doesn't take days to burn!
Essential oil – your choice, but basil or pine is good for prosperity.
Herbs of your choice – but again basil and pine are good for prosperity and poppy seeds are good for money.
A small knife or pin
Slip of paper
Pen
Cauldron or fireproof dish

Take your candle and carve symbols into it that represent prosperity to you, it could be a pound or a dollar sign, it could be a rune or a sigil – go with what works for you.

Then dress the candle with essential oil, work from the centre of the candle up to the top and from the centre down to the bottom, as you dress the candle charge it with your intent.

Then write down your desire for prosperity, abundance, money needed- whatever your particular requirement is on the slip of paper, as you write visualise yourself receiving it.

Sprinkle the herbs on to the candle and then light it spend some time visualising your needs being met. Say:

"As I light this candle flame,
Powers of autumn energy reign,
Prosperity and abundance mine
Come to me, in the quickest time"

Once you have the visualisation set in your mind take the slip of paper and carefully light it in the flame of the candle and drop it into your cauldron or fireproof dish.

Allow the slip of paper and the candle to burn completely, the ashes can be sprinkled to the wind.

Candle Magic Money Spell

What you will need:

A green or gold candle
Optional herbs & crystals:

Jasmine essential oil (for money) or olive oil works well as it represents fertility
Poppy seeds (for money & luck)
Pine needles or pine essential oil (for money)

Malachite crystal (for money & success)
Green tourmaline crystal (money)

Dress your candle with the oils/herbs. To do this you rub the essential oil from the base of the candle to the centre and from the top of the candle down to the centre. Make sure you are placing the oil from the ends of the candle to the centre because you want to draw the energy in to you. Then roll the candle in crushed herbs so they stick to it.

Place the candle in a holder and put the crystals around the base. Light the candle and focus on the intent, visualise prosperity and money coming your way.

Say three times:

"To the Universe help us to be
Good with finances and money
Guide us to financial good
Abundance, prosperity and guidance should
From financial worry set us free
Allow this magic now to be"

Allow the candle to burn out. Never leave a lit candle unattended. Note: If you add oils and/or herbs to a candle keep an eye on it because the flame can flare or spit.

Money Draw Candle Jar Spell

This uses an old jam or pickle jar and a candle to draw money to you.

You will need:

A clean, empty jar with a lid (an old pickle, jam or mason jar is fine)

A small candle that will fit on top. A birthday cake candle is perfect. Green, gold or orange would be good colours as they all represent money and success.
A slip of paper
Pen
Paint or Sharpie pen to draw on the outside of the jar
Dried herbs: Mint, basil, cinnamon or cloves (or a combination)
Dried rice

Using paint or a Sharpie pen, draw a £ sign on the outside of the jar. You can draw more than one if you want to or make a pattern of £ and $ signs. Any images or symbols that you associate with money will work.

Take the pen and write an amount on the slip of paper, make sure it is enough to cover your needs. Fold the paper and pop it in the jar. As you do so say out loud:

"Money, money come to me
Make it fast and make it free
Cash in pounds and quick to see
Money, money come to me"

Now take a pinch of herbs and say the chant out loud again, then drop the herbs into the jar. Repeat this nine times, a pinch of herbs and the chant each time. Nine is a powerful number, it works with the magic of three x three. Now add nine pinches of dried rice, saying the following chant each time:

"Magic of money herbs and prosperity rice
Using the power of thrice times thrice
Fast money, fast luck, fast success is mine
Bring me money by the power of nine"

Put the lid on the jar. Light the candle and drop a bit of hot wax onto the lid and quickly stand the candle in the wax so that it sets firm. Allow the candle to burn out as you say, nine times:

"Fast money come to me, by the power of three times three"

When you are finished dispose of the jar and contents in the trash.

Money Pebbles

I am guessing that we all have a pebble or two in our gardens. Or we can find them when we are out and about. Pebbles align with the element of earth which is all about stability, material things and prosperity. Just sitting outside in the fresh air, the pebbles also soak up energy from the sun. The sun brings power, positive energy, growth and happiness. The humble pebble is a serious magical item!

If you can find pebbles that have a flat surface, they are perfect to write symbols on, which is what we are going to do with this spell.

You will need:

Four pebbles, large enough to write a symbol on
Marker pens, in various colours if possible (or acrylic paint works well too)

Wash and dry your pebbles. Lay them out in front of you. Take the first pebble and draw a pound sign on the top with your pen or paint. Say:

"With the magical element of earth
Symbol of money to bring what it's worth

Add in mighty power of the sun
Work your magic until it is done"

You can just draw a simple pound sign or add in colour and design around it. Maybe a green leaf design to symbolize money growing?

Then repeat with each of the other three pebbles. Draw the same design on each or mix it up a bit and use dollar signs or something else that represents money, prosperity and wealth to you. Say the chant as you work on each one.

When you have all four pebbles finished you will need to place them around your home. Try and get them in each of the four corners of your house. Just pop them on the floor in the corner of the room. Or you might like to place them outside, one either side of your front door to help money come in and then the other two at the back of the house. Placement will depend on the layout of your abode! But try and get them spaced out in a square.

Once all four are in place, say:

"With the placement of all four
Money come to me and more
Magic of the earthy stone
Make my house a money zone
Make it so!"

Leave the pebbles in place and watch the money flow in.

Employment Pebble Spell

This spell uses a pebble to help focus new job energy.

You will need:

A pebble, preferably one that you have collected yourself from a favourite place or you can use a crystal

Sit quietly and focus on the type of job you would like. Hold the stone up to your forehead, where your third eye is. Visualise yourself doing the job you would love, set the scene and walk through a day of work in your mind.

See the interview, see it going well and then focus on the employer offering you the position.

Channel the positive energy, allow it to build and then flow from your forehead into the stone.

You might like to say a chant such as:

"Bringing magical change from the element of earth
Allow the Universe, for me a new job bring forth"

The pebble is now charged with positive job energy. When you sit down to look through the paper or internet for a new job, pop the stone in front of you or hold it in your hand. If you need to write a letter for the position, place the stone on the paper as you write. Once you get an interview don't forget to carry the stone with you in your pocket.

Money Mirror Charm

We could all do with a bit of extra cash now and then, right? This spell makes a sweet little money charm to pop in your purse or bag.

You will need:

A tiny mirror about the size of a coin (like the ones used in crafting)
A small piece of green or gold material (or a colour you associate with money)

Hold the mirror in front of you and tell it what you desire, speak directly into the mirror with your wishes. Repeat your desire three times (or more if you feel the need to). Wrap the mirror in the piece of cloth. Say a chant:

"With blessings of money, wealth and cash
May the universe provide me with what I need
Help me create a money stash"

Pop the charm into your purse or wallet, it works best if it is next to money or where you keep your money.

Re-charge the charm when you have received three unexpected amounts of cash coming in.

Money Magic Mirror Spell

We see mirrors pop up in lots of the fairy tales such as Snow White and Arabian Nights. And they have long been used or working magic, from scrying to see the future to charms, amulets and spell parts. For this spell we are going to use the mirror to help bring money in and to keep it coming.

You will need:

Two small pieces of mirror, the ones you find in craft stores are perfect. They need to be the same size as each other and small enough to pop in your bag. If you can get square ones that is even better as the square shape represents financial stability, but circles are fine too.
Glue or double-sided tape
A small organza or fabric pouch, green, gold or orange in colour works best
Pinch dried basil
Pinch dried mint
A silver coin (such as a 5p piece)

Work this spell on a waxing moon if you can, to add growth energy to your spell. Sit quietly with all the pieces in front of you and begin to visualise money and prosperity coming your way and new ventures or opportunities opening up to you. Take the two mirrors and glue or stick them together back-to-back, so that you have a double-sided mirror.

Now look into one side of the mirror and tell it what you need – this could just be the words 'money' or 'prosperity' but you can be more specific with a figure or something you need to purchase.

Now turn the mirror over and repeat your desire into the other side. Drop the mirror into the pouch and say:

"Magic mirror reflect money to me
Magic mirror bring cash to see"

Now take a pinch of basil and drop it into the pouch, saying:

"Prosperity basil to add cash for me"

Next take a pinch of mint and drop it into the pouch, saying:

"Magic mint to bring money to see"

Then add the silver coin into the pouch and finish by saying:

"Shiny silver, shiny mirror, reflective magic work now for me
Mirror, mirror, silver shine, make the cash now all mine"

Put the pouch into your purse or bag. Or if you have a folder in your home with your bills and invoices in you can pop it in there.

This charm will need recharging with energy by repeating the chants on occasion. I recommend recharging once you have had a couple of windfalls of cash.

Turn Your Luck Around Mirror Spell

We all have periods when we feel that our luck is not helping us, so this spell will turn your luck around. It will also help bring about balance to your life and your finances.

You will need:

Two small mirrors both the same size
Ground nutmeg for luck
A white or light-coloured candle
A black or dark coloured candle
Lighter or matches
Glue
Cord or ribbon

Place both the mirrors under the full moon or at noon under the sun. Light the dark candle and think about money that you owe or areas of your life where you are overwhelmed, or things just aren't working properly.

Now light the white candle from the flame of the black candle. Take some time and allow the light from the white candle to show you a new perspective. What can you do to remove or at least reduce your debts? What areas of your life bring you happiness? Allow solutions or suggestions into your mind to help you bring balance and good fortune back to your life.

Now snuff out the black candle but leave the white candle to burn down safely. Take a pinch of ground nutmeg and sprinkle it onto the mirrors and repeat the chant below four times. Chant:

"Send all negative energy and bad luck away
Bring in balance and good luck today
With the mirror when it does a turn
Abundance, good fortune and luck will return"

Next glue the mirrors together back-to-back sticking a piece of cord or ribbon between them so you can hang them up. Pop the mirror somewhere that you will see it regularly. When you need to change the tide of your luck turn the mirror around whilst saying the chant again.

Throw the black candle stub into the trash.

Peanut Butter Prosperity Spell

Everyone has a jar of peanut butter in their cupboard, don't they? Often it gets forgotten about and pushed to the back. I encourage you to seek it out, don't throw it away, it is packed full of money magic.

You will need:

A peanut butter jar, no need to wash it out, leave the remnants of the peanut butter inside.
A spoonful of honey
A spoonful of porridge oats
A spoonful of uncooked rice
A tea bag

OK, I know this sounds like a breakfast recipe. But all these ingredients work together to create a money magic pot. If you can work your magic on a Thursday, it will bring the added energy of prosperity, wealth and abundance or a Sunday for prosperity, success and wealth. Take the peanut butter jar and remove the lid. Hold the jar in your hands and say:

"Strong and positive magic within the peanut jar
Bring me money, wealth and prosperity from afar
Send abundance down my way
Set this magic in motion today"

Now add the spoonful of honey, this brings prosperity but also helps to make life sweet. Say:

"To make life sweet, I add honey to the jar
Bring me money, wealth and prosperity from afar
Send abundance down my way
Set this magic in motion today"

Then add in the porridge oats, these bring prosperity but also add in fertility for new projects, ventures and avenues of cash flow. Say:

"Prosperity and new possibilities, oats bring to the jar
Bring me money, wealth and prosperity from afar
Send abundance down my way
Set this magic in motion today"

And now the uncooked rice for prosperity of course, but also fertility of ideas and new possibilities with added stability energy.

"Financial stability and money magic, rice adds to the jar
Bring me money, wealth and prosperity from afar
Send abundance down my way
Set this magic in motion today"

Lastly the tea bag, just a regular tea bag filled with black tea. Open the bag and tip the contents into the jar. Black tea leaves bring prosperity but also strength and courage.

"Adding strength to my finances, tea leaves drop into the jar
Bring me money, wealth and prosperity from afar
Send abundance down my way
Set this magic in motion today"

Finally place the lid back onto the jar and close tightly. Say:

"The peanut magic is done
Abundance and prosperity is won"

Place the jar on your altar, mantelpiece or side table, somewhere that you will see it regularly. Let the magic work.

Apple Abundance Magic

There are many foods we can use to work some prosperity magic, apples are one of my favourites to work with as they symbolise love, healing, clarity, knowledge, abundance and spirit work.

You will need:

A nice shiny apple
Water
A cloth
A knife

Wash the apple with water and as you do so, visualise any debts or bills you have being washed away. Now dry the apple with the cloth. As you dry the apple visualise money coming your way and say:

"Abundance of apple, shiny and tart
With this magic I make a fresh start

Money and wealth to come my way
Prosperity now will start from this day"

Then cut the apple in half. Take the point of the knife and carve a pound or dollar sign into the skin on one half of the apple. Eat the other half whilst visualising abundance and prosperity with each bite.

Bury the half with the money sign on, this is as an offering to show your gratitude to the Universe.

Mint Money Spell

You will need:

A peppermint sweet wrapper or bag
Three mint sweets
Dried mint
A pen
Peppermint tea
Sticky tape

Begin by making yourself a cup of mint tea. Next take the mint sweet wrapper or bag and open it out flat. Write the words inside the wrapper, if the bag is plastic, you can write the words on a slip of paper and place that inside instead.

Rolling mint, rolling mint, rolling mint
Bring money to me so I am not skint

Now place each mint sweet into the centre of the wrapper, as you put each one in, say:

"One mint bring money to me

Two mints fast cash to see
Three mints finds prosperity"

Then take a pinch of the dried mint, sprinkling it over the mints and say:

"Rolling mint, rolling mint, rolling mint
Bring money to mint so I am not skint"

Now carefully roll the wrapper up keeping the spell ingredients inside. As you roll, repeat the rolling mint chant three times. Fold the ends over and secure with sticky tape. Now sit quietly drinking your tea, make sure to breath in the aroma and savour the taste and visualise the money rolling in. Pop the mint spell on your altar, mantlepiece or somewhere you will see it regularly.

If you need extra cash hold the mint spell in your hand and repeat the rolling mint chant three times.

Banish Those Bills BBQ

The element of fire is absolutely perfect for banishing with its destructive and cleansing flames, it can literally burn up your debts and bills.

What you need:

A BBQ with smoldering coals
A slip of paper and pen or a credit card bill
Pinch of dried sage

The magic here is simple, all you need to do is write the amount of money you owe onto a slip of paper. Now write over the top of the amount in capital letters 'PAID IN FULL' and drop it onto the hot and smoldering BBQ coals. You could even use your credit card bill or invoices you owe, tear them into pieces and throw them on to burn up.

As you do so visualise your debts disappearing and any money you owe being paid off.

You could even say a chant as you do so, something like:

"With the heat and flames of the coal
Banish my debts and make it my goal
Money comes in to pay the lot
Debts and bills will go with a shot"

Sprinkle a pinch of dried herbs or spices on top to help banish the debts, something like sage would be perfect as it helps clear and cleanse.

Heat Up Your Money Matters

Once you have your BBQ nice and hot you are ready for the food. Lots of different types of food carry the magic of prosperity and abundance so you can tie that in with your meal.

- Pork sausages or pork chops are excellent to bring prosperity and luck, pork is also associated with the element of fire, so it carries a boost of energy too.
- Chucking a beef steak or burger on the BBQ will bring the energy of fertility for new beginnings, projects and new avenues of money, it too carries the element of fire for power and earth for all material things.
- Chicken wings are perfect to BBQ not just for the taste but also because chicken brings prosperity, luck and fertility. A triple whammy of money magic.

- Brush your food with olive oil to add the fertility magic of olives.

Let's not forget the veggies!

- Corn on the cob makes a delicious BBQ addition and corn carries the magic of abundance, luck, prosperity and fertility – that's four hits of money magic coming your way.
- Add onions to your burger and you bring in a fertility hit with the energy of fire to back it up.
- Put a dollop of ketchup on your burger and you add the creativity of tomato which can help you get creative with your money-making ideas.

And for dessert, chargrilled pineapple is fantastic and comes with the added bonus of luck and prosperity magic. Wrap a banana in foil and bake it on the grill and you bring in even more prosperity energy.

Write your wish, a pound symbol or amount of money you need on a large bay leaf and drop it onto the hot coals.

Paint pound signs with vegetable or olive oil onto your burgers or buns before you add them to the grill. Marinate any meats or vegetables in olive oil for fertility and add in money bringing herbs such as mint or basil. Pop in a bit of crushed root ginger to add prosperity and success magic, also aligned with the element of fire it brings an extra manifesting boost.

Leaf Magic

Leaves make a perfect item to use in spells and particularly for money magic. During the autumn fallen leaves are in abundance and they come in all shades of gorgeous colours.

Find the largest fallen leaves that you can, whether it is from your garden or when you are out and about. This spell will help to increase your finances and also reduce your debts using the power of fire. If you are having a bonfire then perfect. Otherwise, you can use a fire pit or set fire to your spell and drop it into a fireproof dish. Please be careful and don't leave fires unattended.

You will need:

3 large fallen autumn leaves
Twine or string (natural so that it burns)
A slip of paper
Pencil
6 cloves
Ground ginger
A fireproof dish or a bonfire
Matches/lighter

Take your largest autumn leaf and lay it out flat in front of you. Place 3 cloves in the centre and say:

"With clove comes spice and heat, my debts now to retreat"

Sprinkle a pinch of ground ginger on top and say:

"Power and creativity with ginger come, money and abundance in a large sum"

Now place the next leaf on top and repeat with the cloves and ginger. When you have your pile of leaves, cloves and ginger write on the slip of paper:

"Money, prosperity and abundance come to me"

Place the slip of paper on the top of your pile. Carefully roll the leaves up with the slip of paper inside and tie it securely with the twine or string.

Your leaf parcel now needs to be burnt. Throw it in a bonfire or fire pit and allow the flames to work their magic. As you toss the parcel into the fire, repeat the chants:

> *"With clove comes spice and heat, my debts now to retreat*
> *Power and creativity with ginger come, money and abundance in a large sum*
> *Money, prosperity and abundance come to me"*

If you don't have a fire, you can light the parcel with a match or lighter and drop it into a fireproof dish. This can be tricky so please be careful. The alternative is to bury the parcel under the soil in your garden, but make sure you have used biodegradable string.

Money Making Leaf Spell

Use any kind of leaf in this spell, one that has the colours of autumn within is preferable.

You will need:

A large fallen autumn leaf
A green candle
An orange candle
Matches or lighter
A felt tip pen or Sharpie
A piece of cardboard or old board

Set the cardboard or board in front of you, this is to provide protection for your table or surface from candle wax. Place the leaf onto the surface. Now write the words 'money, prosperity, abundance' onto the leaf. As you do so visualise money and prosperity coming your way and say:

"Magical abundance of the autumn trees
I ask that the leaf deliver money to me
Power of the trees and magic of the land
Bring money to me, place it in my hand"

Now light the green candle and hold it carefully so that the wax drips onto the leaf, allow enough wax to drip to cover the words, saying:

"Green abundance magic add to the trees
Bringing money right now to me"

Now light the orange candle from the flame of the green one and snuff the green one out.

Repeat by dripping the orange wax over the green, saying:

"Orange success magic add to the trees
Bringing abundance right now to me"

Snuff out the orange candle. Allow the leaf to dry and then place it on your altar, beside your front door or under your door mat to bring abundance and prosperity your way.

Layering Leaf Spell

Draw on the magic of autumn leaves to layer up your finances. Using an orange candle to bring success or green which is all about prosperity. Both colours also reflect the colours found in nature.

You will need:

7 large fallen leaves. Don't pick them from the tree, they need to have naturally fallen, collect them from the ground.
An orange or green candle and a safe holder
Lighter or matches
6 small silver coins
A piece of string or ribbon

Light your candle and set it in front of you. Watch the flame and take a few deep breathes in and out to centre and focus. Now take one of the leaves and lay it out in front of you. Take one of the silver coins and hold it in your hand, charge it with the energy of prosperity and abundance. Say:

"Silver coin bring prosperity to me
Abundance and wealth let me see"

Place the coin in the centre of the leaf. Take another leaf and lay it over the top of the coin. Now charge the second coin by holding it in your hand and saying the chant again. Place it on the leaf.

Repeat this process of leaf, coin, leaf, until you finish with a final leaf. Carefully roll up the pile of leaves and coins and tie it with the string. Say:

"With the colour magic of Mother Nature
Wealth, prosperity and abundance for sure
The power of seven, silver and six
Money will appear right into the mix"

Place the bundle under your front doorstep or above a doorway so that each person coming into the house brings the energy of prosperity in with them.

Leaf Money Symbols

The use of symbols and magical sigils dates a long way back through history. Use the magic of leaves and imbue them with prosperity energy by writing symbols onto them.

You will need:

A large leaf
A felt tip pen/Sharpie
A green candle in a safe holder
Lighter or matches
Cauldron or fireproof dish

Light your candle and watch the flame for a moment. Focus on bringing money into your life. Now take the leaf and your pen. Draw symbols onto the leaf, things that you associate with money. It might be pound or dollar signs. But get creative, you may like to draw images of the sun to represent the powerful manifesting energy of the sun. Growth can be shown by drawing green shoots. Go with your inspiration!

Once you have finished your leaf design, very carefully take the candle and drip a few drops of hot wax onto the leaf, this will 'seal the deal'. Say:

"With the magic of autumn leaves
Money will come straight over to me
A drop of wax to keep it real
Now this is a completely done deal"

Place the candle back safely. Then light the corner of the leaf from the candle flame and drop it into the fireproof dish.

Depending on how dry the leaf is, it may burn quickly or might need to be re-lit a few times.

The ashes can be buried in your garden or thrown to the wind.

Quick Cash Symbols Spell

Using the magic of money symbols this simple spell can be used to bring fast money your way.

You will need:

Pen
Sheet of paper
Envelope

Take your paper and pen and sit quietly for a moment, focus on the money you need urgently. Visualise that money coming to you quickly. Draw a big pound sign in the centre of the paper. Next draw a dollar sign over the top and then a Euro symbol over the top of that. Write the amount of cash you need in numbers above the currency symbols.

Now fill the paper with money symbols. Start at the top left corner of the paper and draw symbols all around the edge, turning the paper as you reach each corner until you have created a frame. Use the infinity sign, four leaf clover and the symbol for Leo as it corresponds with fast cash.

Fold the paper over towards you to bring positive energy in, turn and fold again, then pop it in the envelope. Seal the envelope and write on the front:

Fast cash now, bring to me
Fast cash now, with symbology
Pounds, Dollars, Euros and signs
Bring me money now, make it mine

Say the chant out loud as you write it. Place the envelope somewhere you will see it until the money appears, then you can burn it, bury it or throw it in the trash.

Prosperity Symbol Spell

One of my favourite ways to work with symbols is to carve them into or draw them onto candles. This spell uses that technique to draw money your way.

You will need:

A candle in the colour you associate with money, I like to use green or gold
A safe candle holder
Matches or a lighter
A pin
A pen that will draw on wax such as a Sharpie

I like to work money drawing spells on the waxing or full moon, if you can schedule your spell to coincide with those moon phases it really helps boost the power.

Take your candle and sit quietly focusing on what images or symbols represent money, prosperity and wealth to you. Now take the pen and start to draw the symbols over the outside of your candle. If you prefer you can use the pin to carve them instead. You could use any of the symbols I have mentioned above but trust your intuition and be guided by what symbols come into your mind. The images can be big or small, link them together or give them space. You don't have to be overly artistic for this, just draw what you feel is right. As you do so you might like to chant, something like this:

"Symbols and signs mean money for me
Images and shapes prosperity to see"

Keep drawing until you have covered the entire outside of the candle. Take your pin and push it into the centre of one of the most prominent images that you have drawn. Push the pin in about halfway. Now set your candle into the safe holder. Light the candle.

Repeat your chant again, three times. Sit quietly and watch the candle burn, visualise money coming to you and new opportunities opening up. Watch the candle until the wax melts enough for the pin to drop out from the candle. Once the pin drops your spell is complete.

The remains of the candle can be disposed of in the trash.

Scrying Seed Magic

Scrying is the art of reading the surface of water. This works really well at nighttime if you have the light of the moon, or you can use a candle for the same purpose. We also bring in the prosperity energy of pumpkin seeds which you can save when you scoop out your pumpkins to carve.

You will need:

A candle in a safe holder
A lighter or matches
A bowl, preferably with a dark inside
A jug of water
Handful of pumpkin seeds
Notepad and pen

Work this spell preferably in the evening with the lights turned out. Set your bowl in front of you. Position the candle behind it.Pour some water into the bowl, about three quarters of the way full. Say:

"With the magic of this night
Wisdom of the water make things right
Energy of pumpkin seeds allow me to see
How my finances pan out for me"

Light the candle and make sure the flame is casting flickering light onto the surface of the water. Take a few pumpkin seeds in your hand and say:

"Pumpkin seeds with magic abound
Show me what abundance can be found"

Sprinkle the seeds on top of the water. Take a few slow deep breathes in and out to calm and centre yourself. Now look across the top of the surface of the water, don't stare too intently. Allow your eyes to relax and unfocus. Watch the water as it reflects the candle flame and see what images it casts on the water. Also take note of any shapes or symbols the pumpkin seeds create. You might also hear words or see images in your mind, take note of them.

When you feel you are done, snuff out the candle and tip the water and seeds onto the earth. Make a note of any images, signs or symbols. Think about them over the next couple of days and see what they mean to you in regard to your finances.

Rose Thorn Debt Release Spell

Here we will use thorns to release your debts and petals to bring money in.

You will need:

One rose flower head
Three rose thorns

A slip of paper
Pen
A bowl of water
A pinch of ground cinnamon

Place a bowl of water in front of you. Take the slip of paper and write 'debt' in the centre of it. Now take the rose thorns and push the point of each one through the paper. Say the following each time:

"Sharpness of the rose thorn
Now my debts will be gone"

Now drop the paper with the thorns into the water and say:

"Water release and clear that which I owe"

Then take the rose flower head and gently pull each petal off and drop it into the water, with each petal say:

"Rose abundance bring money to me
Magic of the flower show prosperity"

This may take a while depending on how many petals you have, but as you work with this visualise money coming your way. When you are finished add a sprinkle of ground cinnamon over the top of the dish and say:

"Fiery cinnamon with success and luck
This rose spell with bring me big bucks!"

The water can then be tipped onto your garden, compost or trash.

Plant Prosperity Spell

Use the magic of summer flowers and herbs to bring some prosperity magic into your world.

You will need:

An envelope
Sheet of paper
Pen
Flower petals such as rose or dandelion (use something that is flowering in your garden now)
Herbs such as lemon balm, basil and mint

Take the envelope and write your name on the outside, as you would when you address an envelope to send. Next take sheet of paper and write the following chant on it, three times. As you write, say the chant out loud.

"Prosperity, abundance and money-making powers
Bring these to me with the energy of flowers
Plants that grow now bring to me
Money and wealth for me to see"

Now take the flower petals and sprinkle them into the centre of the paper. As you do so say:

"Flower magic bring to me
Money, abundance and prosperity"

Sit for a moment and look at the colour and shape of the petals and visualise money and abundance coming your way. Next take the herbs, just a few of the leaves will do, sprinkle these on top of the petals and say:

"Money magic, power of herbal green
Bring me prosperity to be seen"

Sit for a moment and look at the colour and shape of the herbs and visualise money and abundance coming your way. Now fold the paper over and over again to seal the plant matter inside the sheet of paper and then put it in the envelope. Hold the envelope in your hands and repeat the first chant you wrote on the paper, say it out loud three times and visualise money coming in.

If you are able to, bury this envelope in the soil in your garden. If not place it outside for the weather to erode.

Pumpkin Prosperity Magic

The tradition of carving pumpkins is an old one, although it began with carved turnips (which is a lot of hard work!). They were used to frighten away evil spirits. However, the pumpkin with its bright orange skin brings success and with the amount of seeds inside it has a whole heap load of money energy. So, let's combine the Halloween pumpkin carving with some prosperity magic.

You will need:

A pumpkin
Carving tools
A clean jar

When you scoop out the seeds of your pumpkin, which is a really icky job! Save the seeds. Rinse them in cold water to get rid of the stringy pumpkin flesh and dry them on a tea towel. Spread the seeds over a large tray and leave them somewhere warm to dry out. When they are fully dry drop them into a clean jar, one or two at a time and chant:

"Prosperity pumpkin seeds
Bring me money for my needs
As the seeds fill up the jar
Abundance from me will never be far"

Pop the jar in your hallway or porch so that you will see it regularly. If you need a boost of cash, give the jar a shake.

There are many pumpkin designs, a lot of which have scary faces. And if you want to carve a face, go right ahead but what about including a money symbol as well? A pound or dollar sign works well, carve it into the front and make it a feature of the pumpkin or just add a small symbol at the back. As you carve visualise money and prosperity coming your way.

Lucky Black Cat

The poor 'ole black cat has a bit of a mixed history. In the past some cultures considered them to be bad luck, and it was often thought that a black cat was an evil witch that had shape shifted. However, the Egyptians worshipped cats in many forms and today the feline is a familiar sight in a lot of households. The black cat has now taken on the role of being lucky, so let's work with that energy. We are using an apple in this spell work too, another symbol of Samhain/Halloween and autumn but also one of abundance and prosperity too.

You will need:

An image, photo, or a paper Halloween decoration of a black cat

An apple
A knife
String or an elastic band

Using the knife, carefully cut the apple in half. Next hold the image of the cat in your hand and say:

"Black cat, black cat, bring your magic to me
Black cat, black cat, shower money to see
Black cat, black cat, bring abundance my way
Black cat, black cat, let me know prosperity today"

Say this chant three times and visualise money coming your way. Then fold the image over until it is small enough to fit inside the apple. Pop the cat image in between both halves of the apple and then tie it together with the string or elastic band. Say:

"Apple set your magic free
Apple bring prosperity to me"

Then bury the apple in your garden or in a pot of soil.

Money Ladder

1st May is traditionally known as May Day, and we often still see the Maypole at local fairs. It has ancient traditions that revolve around fertility so we can use that idea to bring money in. This little spell combines the ribbon idea from the Maypole to use in a very old piece of magic, the Witch Ladder.

The first recorded find of a witches' ladder was in 1886 during the repairs of an old house in Somerset, England. Within the roof space they found a pile of broomsticks, an old chair and a length of braided cord, with a loop at one end and lots of cockerel feathers threaded through the braid.

Over the years there have been many theories as to the purpose of the braid but the most popular seems to be that the ladder was for cursing. With ideas ranging from curdling the milk from a neighbour's cow through to wishing someone dead. Other ideas suggest that it was used for healing or casting wishes. The fact is that nobody really knows.

The witch ladder is one of my favourite magical tools and they are seen nowadays in many forms but all usually with the basic braid of three cords together with feathers in between often nine of them. I also like to add sprigs of herbs to mine and a bit of colour magic in the form of ribbons.

You will need:

> Cut nine pieces of natural twine or ribbon (or a mixture of both), about 1 metre in length.
> Feathers, charms or sprigs of herbs
> If you are going to use ribbon rather than twine, then think about colour too. Pick the colour to match the intent of your witch's ladder, I would go with green or orange to represent prosperity and success.

Gather together three strands and tie a knot in one end, then begin to plait together tying a knot at the other end when you have finished. Repeat with the other strands until you have three sets of three plaited lengths. Then you are going to plait these together. While you are working focus on your intent, chant as you go:

"With the power of three times three
Money and abundance may you come to me
With the power of May Day magic bring
Prosperity and success this spring"

If you are really crafty you can add in beads, charms or other embellishments. Or if you are like me, sew them on afterwards. Once you have your completed plait, make sure it is secure at both ends. Then at regular intervals poke in a feather or piece of herb between the braiding. As you do this focus on the intent.

Place your finished witches' ladder somewhere you will see it every day until your purpose has come to fruition.

Ribbon Knot Magic

The use of knot magic is ancient, but it is brought up to date here with a coloured ribbon magical spell to bring about money. Tying knots in the ribbon is a form of binding your desire into the spell. Traditionally nine knots are made, each knot bringing you closer to your goal.

You will need:

> A piece of ribbon in a colour you associate with money and wealth, my choice would be green but orange and gold work well too.
> This works best on a new, waxing or full moon as the power of these moon phases helps draw money to you.

Sit quietly and visualise money coming your way. Now take the ribbon in your hands and tie a knot near to one end of the ribbon. As you tie the first knot say:

> *"By the knot of one this spell has begun, £10"*

Then tie your second knot and say:

> *"By the knot of two this spell will come true, £20"*

Tie your third knot and say:

"By the knot of three, so shall it be, £30"

Onto your fourth knot and say:

"By the knot of four, it is strengthened more, £40"

For your fifth knot, say:

"By the knot of five, so may it thrive, £50"

And your sixth knot, say:

"By the knot of six, this spell is fixed, £60"

Tie your seventh knot and say:

"By the knot of seven, be it powered by the heavens, £70"

Now tie your eighth knot and say:

"By the knot of eight, guide the hand of fate, £80"

Lastly tie your ninth knot and say:

"By the knot of nine, the money is mine, £90"

Place the cord in a safe place or carry it with you. Then when you need some money in a hurry untie one or more of the knots and wait for the money to come in. Un-tying the knot releases the magic.

You can state any amount of money for each knot, it doesn't need to be in ten-pound increments.

Cord Cutting & Knot Tying Money Spell

What you will need:

A piece of sewing thread – something that can be burnt
A piece of string, wool, twine or ribbon
A black candle and a white candle in safe holders
A lighter or matches
A fireproof mat or board

Tie one end of the thread around the white candle, this represents you. Tie the other end of the thread to the black candle, this represents your debts. Place them on a safe surface that won't be damaged. Light the white candle first then the black one. Say:

"See the thread that binds me to my debt
Now I cut the cords, so they are met
Release me now, free me and let go
My connection to debt is removed, make it so"

Watch the candles until the flame lights the thread and snaps the connection. When the thread burns through see your debts disappearing and feel the relief as they do so. Now you can snuff out the candles. These can be placed in the trash. Take your piece of string or ribbon and tie three knots in it, each time you tie a knot say:

"My release from debt is done
Now more money to me will come
I tie this knot to keep safe my cash
Prosperity will come now with a dash"

Hang the knotted string above your doorway or place it on your altar. If it is smaller, you could pop the knotted string in your purse or handbag.

Earthy Knot/Cord Magic

Long stems of grass really lend themselves to knot magic as do climbing plants such as ivy and they carry the added energy of the element of earth. But you can also use garden twine, string or ribbon.

If you want a new job, a new dress or maybe a holiday, pick your intent and tie the energy into a knot. Tie a knot with the intent of prosperity, good health and luck and hang it over your front door so that every time someone walks in, they bring the positive energy with them.

If you are crafty you can of course take the knot magic a step further and crochet, weave or knit energy into something beautiful by putting the magic in as you create. As you tie each knot, crochet or knit a stitch, you could add in a chant, such as:

"With this magical knot/stitch I weave
Abundance, wealth and prosperity"

Or

"With this magical knot/stitch I weave
A holiday and plenty of spending money for me"

Tailor the chant to the intent that you want to create.

String Magic for Money Making

This is a really simple spell to increase your finances using odd bits of string, ribbon or yarn. You start this spell off and then it becomes an ongoing project with you adding magic to it on a regular basis. This continuing energy will keep money coming into you.

You will need:

A clean jar (jam, pickle, decorative, whatever you feel drawn to use)

A lid for the jar
A pinch of dried mint
A pinch of dried basil
Odd pieces of yarn or string

Place the jar in front of you and say:

"Jar of glass, magic within
Let this prosperity spell begin"

Now take the pinch of dried mint and add it to the jar, saying:

"Prosperity magic that mint brings
Now this prosperity spell begins"

Next add the pinch of dried basil to the jar, saying:

"Abundance magic that basil brings
Now this prosperity spell begins"

Then take a short piece of yarn or string and tie a knot in it, saying:

"Money magic come to me
The knot now seals it for all to see"

Drop the string into the jar. Put the lid on the jar and place it somewhere you will see it daily. On a regular basis, tie a knot into another piece of string and repeat the chant, dropping it into the jar and replacing the lid. You can do this on a daily or weekly basis. Once the jar is full you can tip the contents into the trash (or compost bin if the items are biodegradable). And re-start the jar.

Prosperity Talisman

What is a talisman? Well, it is a magically charged object that attracts a desired energy. Talismans bring power and energy to the wearer. In this case we can charge it with energy to bring about prosperity, luck and abundance.

You will need:

A white candle (or colour of your choice)
A quartz or similar boosting/amplifying crystal (if you have one), this could be a clear crystal quartz, pyrite, obsidian, malachite, bloodstone or a piece of gold jewellery. You don't need this to work the spell successfully but if you have it in place it helps to boost the power of the spell and the speed with which it works.
A crystal or piece of jewellery to use as your talisman

Place the boosting crystal (if using) in front of the candle and light the candle wick. Hold your talisman crystal or piece of jewellery in your hands and visualise your intent/goal/desire – see money coming in, bills being paid easily and abundance within your life. Now send that energy into your talisman. Visualise all the good stuff entering into the crystal or piece of jewellery, see it as a magnet that attracts money and wealth.

When ready place your talisman so that it touches the base of the booster crystal or the base of the candle. You might like to say a chant:

"Crystal energy and magical power
Charge this talisman this hour
Attract and bring money direct to me
Abundance now and prosperity"

Leave the crystal there until the candle has burnt out, or for at least an hour (do not leave lit candles unattended). Then your talisman is good to go, carry it with you or wear it. You can layer this spell by burning a corresponding incense or passing the talisman through the smoke. You can also dress the candle in a matching oil blend and/or sprinkle with dried herbs such as basil or mint. Or carve symbols into the candle with a pin, pound or dollar signs work well.

Tarot Money Magic

Tarot cards are normally used in readings to provide guidance and insight. Tarot cards can also be used in spell workings. Some of them are particularly useful to help draw money to you. If you don't own a set of tarot cards, you can print an image from the net and use that in this spell instead.

You will need:

Three tarot cards:

Six of Wands – this card symbolises an amount of unexpected cash coming your way
Nine of Pentacles – is all about having the material items you want in abundance
Ace of Pentacles – brings new opportunities for prosperity

Three candles in a colour that suggests prosperity and money to you, I would work with green, orange and gold.
Candle holders
Lighter or matches
A pin or sharp knife

Take each of your candles in turn and carve a pound or dollar symbol into the side using a pin or sharp knife. If you have a pumpkin carving tool that would work well too. Place them in holders in front of you in a row. Now take each of the tarot cards and place them down, one in front of each candle. Light the candle behind the Ace of Pentacles and say:

"Ace of Pentacles, magic of tarot now
Open new money-making opportunities, show me how"

Next light the candle behind the Nine of Pentacles and say:

"Nine of Pentacles, magic of tarot card
Bring abundance to me, don't make it hard"

Light the candle behind the Six of Wands and say:

"Six of Wands, magic of tarot power
Prizes of money and cash now shower!"

Sit quietly and watch the candle flames and study the images on each of the cards. Be open to any messages that come your way. Allow the candles to burn out completely. Pop the three tarot cards on your altar, mantlepiece or somewhere you will see them regularly, leave them up until the money magic begins to manifest.

Tarot Card Cash Spell

This spell works with the focused energy of several tarot cards and adds in the magic from a candle spell.

You will need:

A green, gold or orange candle in a safe holder

Lighter or matches
Wheel of Fortune tarot card
Ace of Pentacles tarot card
The Chariot tarot card
The World tarot card
The Empress tarot card

On a safe flat surface set the candle in a holder in front of you but leave space to lay the cards down in front of the candle. Light the candle and say:

"Power of magic within the tarot card
Bring me prosperity but don't make it hard
Read the cards and bring what may
Let no obstacles stand in my way"

First lay down the Chariot card and sit quietly looking at the images, state out loud:

"The Chariot to set things in motion"

Take some time to see money coming to you and action starting to happen to improve your prosperity and abundance. When you are ready lay down the Wheel of Fortune card next to the Chariot and sit quietly looking at the images, state out loud:

"The Wheel of Fortune to open up new opportunities"

Take some time to visualise new ventures and avenues opening up to you. When you are ready lay down the Ace of Pentacles and sit quietly looking at the images, state out loud:

"The Ace of Pentacles for abundance and prosperity"

Take some time to visualise money and abundance coming your way. When you are ready lay down the Empress card next to the others. Sit quietly and look at the images, state out loud:

"The Empress for financial growth"

Take some time to visualise your finances growing and expanding. Lastly lay down the World card, taking some time to really look at the images, state out loud:

"The World to bring me success"

Spend some time visualising your ultimate financial goal happening.

Now look at all the cards together and see if anything jumps out at you in particular, part of an image or one of the cards specifically, there may be a message for you. When you are ready, finish up by saying:

"Tarot magic come to me
Prosperity and financial stability
Cards of tarot bring this energy
By my will so mote it be"

Snuff out the candle and set the cards on your altar or mantel where you will see them. If you feel the spell is working too slowly you can relight the candle later and say the last chant three times to boost the magic. Once the spell has worked you can dispose of the candle and put the cards back into the deck.

Lucky Number Spell

We can work magic with numbers to bring money, abundance and prosperity your way. I like to add in coins because they represent money obviously but because they also involve the use of numbers.

You will need:

Five coins – a penny, two pence x 2, five pence x 2
A green candle in a holder
Matches or lighter

We will work with five coins to draw upon the energy of number five to bring good positive changes to your finances. Using different denominations of coins add more number magic. Light your candle, green is good for prosperity, but you could use a gold or orange one. Focus on the flame and hold all five coins in your hand. Say:

"Money magic, numbers free
Bring prosperity and money quick to me"

Now lay the coins out in front of the candle, 'tails up' so that you can see the number value on each coin. Lay them starting with the penny, then the two pences followed by the fives, left to right. Now pick up the penny and say:

"With the magic of number one
Keep my finances secure, now tis done"

Turn the penny over and place it back down.
Pick up both two pence coins and say:

"Magic of the number two
Bring about balance and abundance true"

Turn them both over and place them back down
Then pick up the two five pence coins and say:

"Magic of the number five
Prosperity and money will now arrive"

Turn them both over and place them back down Now sit quietly for a moment and focus on the candle flame, visualise money and prosperity coming your way along with new opportunities. Allow the candle to burn out safely.

Then take the coins and stack them up on top of each other, place this pile of coins somewhere safe. On a hall table, bedside table, altar or mantelpiece. Leave them there until the magic has worked. You can also repeat this spell if you need to bring in more cash.

Numbers Spell

You will need:

A piece of paper
A pen or pencil
A green, orange or gold candle in a safe holder
Lighters or matches
Sharp knife, skewer or needle
Cauldron or fireproof dish

Take your candle and carefully carve the number 8 into the wax using the tip of a sharp knife, a skewer or a large needle. Visualise money coming your way as you do so and repeat the chant eight times:

Magic number eight in numerology
Bring now to me, abundance, money and prosperity

Set the candle in a safe holder and light the wick. Next take the sheet of paper and pen and write the word 'eight' on the paper at the top, say the chant, then write the word 'eight' again below the first one and say the chant. Repeat this until you have the word 'eight' written eight times and you have said the chant eight times. Visualise money coming to you as you write. Now draw the figure '8' around the edge of the paper eight times, repeating the chant again eight times over.

Now fold the paper towards you and draw the figure '8' on the outside, eight times repeating the chant after each figure. Then catch the paper alight from the flame of the candle and drop it safely in the cauldron to burn.

The ashes can be thrown to the winds, buried in the garden or placed in the trash. Keep an eye out for the number eight appearing in everyday life, it could be a sign!

Money Draw Spray

Make yourself a spritzer spray to use to bring money draw energy into your home by spraying it around each room. Or spray a little on your hands before you fill in your lottery ticket. Spritz a little into your purse or wallet to bring money in quickly.

Basic spritz recipe:

90ml/3 fl oz distilled water
12 drops essential oil
Spray/spritzer bottle

To make distilled water, boil water in your kettle and allow it to cool. Pop the water and the oils into a spray bottle and give it a little shake. Hold the bottle in both hands and visualise money coming to you. See your bank account or savings account increasing. Say:

"Power of oils bring your money draw in
Prosperity and cash come to me or even a win"

I like to use peppermint or cinnamon essential oil. Peppermint is a real money draw oil and cinnamon brings about success in all things. A combination of the two would be perfect. It will also smell delicious. The oils can also be used in a diffuser.

Spritz into the air in each room in your house, paying particular attention to any doorways as they are entry ways that 'bring' energy in. Say the chant as you spray each room.

Bath Prosperity Ritual Spell

One of the best ways to relax and pamper yourself is to take a nice soothing bath. Not only does this help your energy levels and state of mind, but it can also be used to work magic. If you are feeling frazzled and stressed it makes a barrier for positive energy to come your way. By working with a bath ritual spell, you can relax and cleanse your body, mind and spirit and also bring in the good stuff.

You will need:

A nice hot bath
Candles if you have the room
2 tablespoons dried herbs, spices or flowers
A square of fabric and ribbon or a pouch with ties
10 drops essential oil
1 tablespoon sea salt

With the choice of herbs, I would recommend you trust your intuition and take a look in your herb and spice rack and see what appeals to you. Do make sure it is OK to use on your skin though. I would recommend dried mint, not only does it carry prosperity magic, but it is cleansing too. A cinnamon stick broken in half also works well for the scent and it brings a good punch of success magic. Dried basil is also excellent for bringing the money in.

Take each ingredient in your hands and charge it with the intent of bringing prosperity magic to you. Say:

"Money magic come to me
Bring the cash and make me debt free
Power of herbs, energy of spice now
Abundance and prosperity show me how"

Put each ingredient, into the pouch or fabric and tie it tightly.

Run yourself a nice hot bath and if you have the space to do so safely, add some candles in the bathroom.

As the water is running you will need to add your magical ingredients. Start with the tablespoon of sea salt, hold it in your hands and visualise cleansing, purifying energy. You need to clear any blockages to allow the positive prosperity energy to come your way. Say:

"Cleansing, purifying energy of salt, release blockages and let them go
Clear them out with the magic of salt I now throw"

Drop the salt into the bath and give the water a swirl around. Then drop the pouch of herbs and spices into the water and repeat the money magic chant.

Step into the water and relax. Take some time to visualise negative energy being released and opening up to abundance freely coming your way.

When you are finished with the bath, the pouch can be discarded.

Sing a Song of Sixpence

OK we want a bit more than sixpence but working with songs that sing about money can really boost your prosperity efforts. There are a whole host of songs out there old and new that draw upon the idea of money. I bet you can name at least two or three off the top of your head. If you need to do some research, the internet will throw up a whole list for you.

You will need:

A means of playing music out loud, your phone, laptop or record player!
A song that sings about money
A green or gold candle in a safe holder
Lighter and matches
Pin or sharp knife

Start by putting the music nice and loud, you will probably need to put the song on repeat as this will take a little time to complete.

Take the candle and the pin or sharp knife. You need to carve the symbol of a pound sign (or something else that symbolises money to you) into the side of the candle, about three quarters of the way up towards the top.

As you carve listen to the words of the song. If you know them, sing along. Place the candle in a safe holder in front of you and light the wick.

Sit for a moment and watch the flame, visualise money coming to you and listen to the words of the song. Allow the music to wash over you.

Really take in the beat of the song. Now we need to raise that magical money energy. Start singing along as loud as you can, feel the energy of the song. If you are able, get up and dance to the beat. Singing and dancing really helps to raise energy. Keep an eye on the candle and when it has burnt down to the pound sign you can direct that energy. Visualise all the singing and dancing energy you have raised spiralling up and out into the universe. As you send it on its way say, "music magic send money to me, music magic let me see". Take a few deep breaths to calm down and clap your hands three times, this will release any excess energy and will help you to ground.

Allow the candle to burn out safely along to the sounds of the song.

Song Word Coin Spell

This spell works using the magic of song words combined with the prosperity energy of silver coins.

You will need:

Song words printed or written out on a sheet of paper.
Pick a song that contains lyrics about money.
Three silver coins, 5p coins work well for this
A piece of sticky tape

Print out the song lyrics, this can be easily done from the internet. Alternatively, you can hand write them out onto a sheet of paper. Sit quietly and read or sing the lyrics to yourself. Focus on the parts that talk specifically about money, as you read or sing them, visualise money and abundance coming your way. Now lay the sheet of paper out in front of you. Take the three silver coins in your hand and say:

"Energy of silver coins and the power of three
Music magic bring money straight to me"

Place one of the coins in the centre of the lyric paper. Repeat the chant.

Place the second coin to the left of the centre one. Repeat the chant.

Place the third coin to the right of the centre one so that you have three silver coins lying in a row in the centre of the song word lyric paper.

Now fold the top of the paper towards you over the coins. Fold the right-hand side of the paper over the centre and the left-hand side across that. Then take the bottom of the paper and fold it upwards over the coins.

You will have created a paper parcel with the coins in the centre. Take the piece of sticky tape and use it to seal the outer flap. As you place the sticky tape say:

> *"Sticky tape to seal the deal".*

Place this coin parcel under your front door mat. As people come into your house the energy and movement will activate the magic to bring money in. If you can't place it under a door mat, pop it somewhere safe, as close to your front door as you can.

The Colour of Money Spell

You will need:

Green pencil, crayon or pen
Sheet of paper
Pinch of dried basil
Pinch of dried mint

Green candle in a safe holder
Lighter or matches
Fireproof dish or cauldron

Set all the items out in front of you. Light the candle and say:

"As I light the candle of green
Prosperity magic now to be seen"

Lay the sheet of paper out in front of you and pick up your writing implement. Focus on what symbols or images mean money to you. It might be pound or dollar signs; it could be numbers. Allow your imagination to run free and start drawing on the sheet of paper. You don't need to be artistic, just go with the flow. As you draw/write visualise money flowing freely into your bank account. Fill the sheet from edge to edge with your symbols, you can even overlap some if you wish. Once you are done the whole page should be filled with green writing and symbols. Hold the finished paper up in front of you and say:

"With the power and symbols of green
Prosperity magic now to be seen"

Lay the paper back down and take your dried herbs. Add a pinch of basil into the centre of the paper and say:

"Abundance and money magic of basil green
Prosperity magic now to be seen"

Add a pinch of mint into the centre of the paper and say:

"Abundance and money magic of peppermint green
Prosperity magic now to be seen"

Then fold the paper from the top to the centre and from the bottom up to the middle then fold the left- and right-hand sides in so that it forms a parcel.

Carefully take the parcel and light the edge from your candle flame and drop it into the fireproof dish. As it burns visualise money flowing freely to you. Once it is burnt say:

"Abundance and prosperity magic of green
Now it is time for the money to be seen"

Allow the candle to burn out safely. The ashes can be thrown into the trash or sprinkled on your garden.

Coin Spell

The idea of green being associated with prosperity could well be that paper money was often green in colour (dollar bills, the old pound notes etc). Silver coins also work really well in money spells. You draw on the power of the colour silver in bringing finances and prosperity but also the symbolism of the coin itself.

You will need:

3 silver coins (5p, 10p, 20p, 50p – it doesn't matter what denomination).
A piece of paper
A pen – green or silver ink would be excellent as it adds another layer of magic
A small piece of sticky tape

Wash the coins under running water and wipe them dry, this releases any negative energy that might have attached itself. Give them a little polish so they are nice and shiny. Take your piece of paper and write:

Silver coins the magic you bring
Make my bank account sing
Prosperity, wealth and abundance my way
Bring in the money as fast as you may

Now draw a large pound or dollar sign over the top of your words. Turn the paper a quarter turn (45 degrees) and draw another pound or dollar sign over the top of your writing again. Turn the paper a quarter turn again and draw another pound or dollar sign over the writing. Then place the silver coins in the centre of the paper, on top of each other. Say the chant out loud:

"Silver coins the magic you bring
Make my bank account sing
Prosperity, wealth and abundance my way
Bring in the money as fast as you may"

Now wrap the coins up, folding the paper so that the coins are safely inside. Seal the parcel with a small piece of sticky tape. Place your coin parcel under your front door mat, under the front doorstep or hide it as close to your front door as you can. The idea is that as people step into your home, they activate the magic and bring prosperity and abundance into your home with them.

All That Glitters

You will need:

5 silver coins (5 pence coins work well)
Aluminium foil – 8cm square piece
Glitter (optional)
Pencil

I like to do this adding in the power of the sun, it brings a boost of magical solar energy which carries a huge punch of abundance zing. Give the coins a bit of a wash and buff to make them as shiny as possible.

I have used the number 8 for the piece of aluminium foil as 8 is a good number for prosperity and abundance magic. Bringing in the energy of the elements helps in all kinds of areas to bring money to you.

If possible, work with this outside in the sunshine, otherwise sit by a window so you can see the sun. Lay the foil out in front of you and draw a five-pointed start on the foil, a pentagram with the top point uppermost. Take the first coin and hold it up to the sun, say:

"Silver coin shining bright
Element of Water bring in your might
The flow of money in a run
Charged with the energy of the sun"

Place the coin to the right-hand point of the star. Take a second coin and hold it up to the sun, say:

"Silver coin shining bright
Element of fire bring in your might
Creative money energy bring some
Charged with the energy of the sun"

Place the coin to the bottom right-hand point of the star. Pick up the third coin and hold it up to the sun, say:

"Silver coin shining bright
Element of Earth bring in your might
Financial stability is now done
Charged with the energy of the sun"

Place the coin to the bottom left-hand point of the star. Pick up the fourth coin and hold it up to the sun, say:

"Silver coin shining bright
Element of air bring in your might
Intellect and financial deals done
Charged with the energy of the sun"

Place the coin to the left-hand point of the star Finally take the last coin and hold it up to the sun, say:

"Silver coin shining bright
Element of spirit bring in your might
Complete the circle now it is done
Charged with the energy of the sun"

Place the coin at the top point of the star. Leave the coins under the sun for at least an hour to charge, longer if you can. Then pile the coins up in the centre of the foil and wrap the foil around them. This can be carried in your bag or pocket to keep the prosperity energy working.

Colour Magic Prosperity Spell

When working with colour magic you add extra layers to the energy of the spell. Each item with a corresponding colour brings another oomph of magic. See how many items you can bring the colour in with when working this candle magic spell.

What you need:

Green cloth
Green candle in a holder
Orange candle in a holder
Green crystal such as green aventurine or malachite
Greenery, any seasonal green leaves
Mint – fresh or dried

Basil – fresh or dried
Vase filled with water
Lighter or matches

Start by setting the scene and lay out your green cloth onto a flat surface such as a tabletop.

Now place your vase of water at the back. Take each piece of greenery and hold it in your hand, say:

"With the magic of nature's gift
Bring my finances a much needed lift
Greenery all fresh and bright
Prosperity and abundance come in with might"

Then place the greenery into the vase. Repeat with the mint and basil if you are using fresh herbs and add them to the vase. Now set your green and orange candles in front of the vase. If you have dried herbs these can be sprinkled onto and around the candle instead but use the same chant as you do so. Take the green crystal in your hands and say:

"Green crystal filled with magic and light
Bring prosperity with all your might"

Place it in front of the candles.
Light the green candle and say:

"Green candle bring fast money to me
Prosperity and abundance let me see"

Light the orange candle and say:

"Orange candle bring lots of success
Abundance and wealth to clear my debts"

Now sit quietly and watch the flames of the candles for a moment Then visualise money and abundance coming your way, see your debts disappearing and financial opportunities opening up for you. Allow the candles to burn out safely.

Place the vase of greenery in a prominent position in your home. Each time you walk past it, visualise money coming to you. When the greenery is past its best, dispose of in the compost or bury it in the garden. The crystal can be popped into your purse or bag.

Whiter Than White

I love to work with colour magic and for me, the new year or new beginnings of any kind work well using the colour white. It is literally a blank canvas, a blank sheet, a blank whatever it might be, open to new and exciting opportunities. This spell draws upon the new and fresh energy of white to bring money your way.

You will need:

A white tablecloth, tea towel or scarf
White candle in a safe holder
Small white dish or plate
Matches or lighter
Spoonful of sugar
Spoonful of white flour

Lay your white cloth on a flat surface. Place your white candle in front of you in its holder, place it on the plate or small dish. Light the wick of the candle, sit quietly focusing on the flame and say:

"New beginnings, fresh new start
Open up opportunities to me, my wish from the heart

Prosperity, abundance and wealth come to me
Avenues for making money allow me to see"

Now take the sugar and sprinkle it around the base of your candle in the dish or plate you have set it upon. As you do so, say:

"Sugar, sprinkled, white and sweet
Bring new money-making opportunities complete"

Now take the white flour and sprinkle it around the base of your candle, in the dish or plate you have set it upon. As you do so, say:

"White flour, fresh with the energy to grow
Open up prosperity and allow money to flow"

Sit quietly and allow the candle to burn out, as you watch the flame visualise new opportunities for money making, prosperity and abundance opening up to you.

The sugar and flour can then be sprinkled on the ground.

Building Your Bank Account

The idea for this spell comes from the old folk tale of a crow adding stones to a jug of water to raise the level of it. Crows are incredibly intelligent birds, so we will be following their example!

You will need:

An empty jar
A handful of pebbles, stones or shingle
A jug of water
A Sharpie or marker pen

Take your empty jar and using a pen draw a line about three quarters of the way up. Write the amount of money you need to bring in alongside the line. If you don't have a figure in mind and just want to increase your general income draw a pound sign beside the line instead.

Now take the jug of water and pour water into the jar to fill it half full. Hold the jar in your hands and say:

"Power of water flow free
Prosperity and abundance come to me"

Next take a pebble and drop it into the water in the jar.

As you do so visualise your bank account growing and money coming into you from new avenues. Say:

"Money, money come to me
Water flow, so mote it be"

Take another pebble and repeat the process, drop it into the water and say the chant.

Repeat this until the water level reaches the line you drew on the side of the jar. Finally say:

"Water magic is now done
I am open to money, let it come"

You can leave the jar on a shelf or out in your garden for a few days to let the magic work.

Once money starts coming in you can tip the water onto the ground.

Currency Cash In

If you have ever travelled abroad, you will know that you usually come home with a purse full of currency that you can't use. Sometimes it is a small amount that isn't worth cashing in or it might be coins that can't be changed. Use that currency to work money magic with. Even if you don't have any foreign currency, you can work this spell using UK coins or notes. If you don't want to waste notes, you can print off images from the internet or use toy money. The important thing here is that you have a visual representation of cash, it doesn't matter if it is real or not.

You will need:

Foreign currency, toy money or printed off images of money
An empty jar with a lid
Three tablespoons sugar
Three tablespoons honey
A handful of sand or earth
A small green or gold candle (birthday candles are excellent for this)
Matches or lighter

Place all the items out in front of you. Take the empty jar and place the currency inside, it doesn't matter if it is notes or coins. As you do so, say:

"Easy cash, fast money, currency I see
Easy cash, fast money, bring it all to me"

Now add the sugar (the amount can be teaspoons or tablespoons depending on the size of jar, the important part is the number 3). As you add the sugar visualise money coming in and say:

"With the power of number three, sugar added to make life sweet"

Next add the honey (the amount can be teaspoons or tablespoons depending on the size of jar, the important part is the number 3). With the power of number three, honey added to draw money to me. Then add in the handful of sand or soil and say:

The element of earth to manifest, money and prosperity at its best

Now put the lid on the jar and give it a shake. Carefully light the candle and allow a few drops of wax to drip on the lid and then set the candle on top of the jar lid. Allow the candle to burn out, keep an eye on it. Once the candle has burn out put the jar somewhere you can see it and every day for three days give it a shake and visualise money coming to you.

On the fourth day smash the jar (somewhere safely, the sink is a good option) and throw the broken pieces into the trash. Please wrap the broken glass carefully before disposing of.

This allows the energy to be released into the Universe.

Folklore Money Spell

This spell brings together several folk traditions associated with money and abundance.

You will need:

9 silver coins (5p or 20p coins work well)
A soft cloth
Peppermint tea bag (or a few sprigs of fresh mint)
Bowl of warm water

Place all the items in front of you on a flat surface. Add the peppermint tea bag to your bowl of warm water. Swirl the mint around with your fingers and say:

"Peppermint with the power of air
Prosperity and abundance now fair
Money will be drawn to me
Wealth and cash for all to see"

Once the mint has infused the water, it should take on a faint colour and you are ready for the coins. Take one of the coins and dip it into the water, repeat the chant. Dry the coin with the soft cloth, make it as shiny as you can. Repeat with the other coins, one at a time, dipping into the water and saying the chant. Once you have cleaned all nine coins, lay them on a windowsill so the light of the moon can shine onto them. Do this on a new, waxing or full moon as this will add increasing energy to the power of the coins. Leave them over night. The next day take the coins in your hand and say:

"Folk lore magic, silver is king
Coins of the realm abundance to bring"

Place each of the coins in and around your home. I would suggest trying to get one coin in each of the four compass directions of your home. One can be placed under the door mat or near the front door. Place one near the back door as well. Windowsills are also excellent spots to place a coin, tuck it out of the way. You could also bury one in your garden, as close to the house as possible.

Once all nine coins have been placed around your home, sit quietly in the centre of your home. Visualise money and abundance coming your way. Repeat the chant nine times:

"Folk lore magic, silver is king
Coins of the realm abundance to bring"

Now forget the coins are there, they will work their magic. Once you feel that the energy is waning you can retrieve the coins and repeat the process of washing them and recharging the magic.

Spider Web Abundance Spell

We are going to use the magic of the web to improve your prosperity, abundance and increase the money coming into your bank account.

You will need:

A sheet of paper and a pen or a spider web image printed from the internet
Reel of thread, black if possible
Black candle in safe holder
Matches or lighter
Cauldron or fireproof dish

Sit comfortably at a table or desk and place the sheet of paper in front of you. Now place the candle in a safe holder so that the paper is between you and the candle. Light the candle.

Quietly focus on the candle flame for a moment and visualise a spider sitting in the middle of a large web. Watch the threads of the web and see how the web expands outwards from the centre, the spider has created its own world in a way that it wants it to be.

Now take your pen and draw a large spider web on your sheet of paper. Start with a cross drawn from edge to edge, then set another cross at right angles to the first. Now draw a circle in the centre, then another a bit further out and another, keep drawing circles over the top of the crosses with a gap between each until you come to the edge of the paper. Once you are finished look at the web, this is your world, now let's create some abundance in it.

Take the pen and write words in the gaps of the web, make them all positive ones that focus on bringing things to you. Words such as 'prosperity', 'abundance', 'wealth' and 'money' work well but you could add in other things that you want/need such as 'good health'.

Fill up all the gaps in the web with your manifesting words, you can repeat the same words.

Once you are done sit back and look at the web you have created, visualise all these things manifesting and coming to you. Say:

Magic and mystery of the spider and web
My destiny is created and these words are said
Positive energy bring these things into be
Spider and web energy work magic for me

Now roll the sheet of paper up. Take the thread and begin to wind it around the scroll of paper, just enough to secure it properly, finish it by tying a knot. Hold the edge of the scroll to the candle flame and set it alight. Carefully drop it into the fireproof dish and allow it to burn out. As it burns say the chant once again.

The ashes can be buried in the garden or thrown to the winds.

Word Spell for Wealth

This spell uses the power of the written and spoken word. You can add the candle if you wish, it rounds the spell up nicely, but it is not essential.

You will need:

A piece of paper
A pen
Optional:

Candle and holder
Matches or lighter
Cauldron or fireproof dish

If using, set the candle in front of you and light the wick.

Take the pen and write at the top edge of the paper.

Money, money, come to me, abundance and wealth for me to see. Now turn the paper clockwise one turn and write along the edge.

> Abundance, wealth and cash for free, Universe I ask you to provide for me

Turn the paper clockwise again and write along the new edge.

> Cash, currency and credit needed now, abundance of the universe show me how

Turn the paper clockwise again to the new top edge and write

> Prosperity, bring it over here, money enough for us to share

Turn the paper clockwise again and you will be back to the edge you began with.

There should be a blank space in the centre of the paper, fill that space with words that bring the energy you need. So, you might use:

> Money, prosperity, cash, pay rise, lottery win, abundance and wealth

Write as many as you like to fill up the space. Visualise your goal as you write. Now fold the paper over, top edge towards you. Then fold the sides in. You can now put this in your bag, purse, wallet or in the drawer you keep your paperwork in. Or you can light the paper from the flame of the candle and allow it to burn out in the cauldron.

Snuff the candle out when you have finished if you use it.

Snow and Ice Money Spell

As snow and ice are variations on frozen water, they carry all the magical properties that water does such as healing, cleansing and purifying and it is a very feminine energy. But because they are water in a transformed state, they also bring the energy of transformation. You can draw upon this transformation power and apply it to your money situation.

You will need:

Snow or ice in a bowl or jug (if the weather isn't providing this you could use ice cubes from the freezer)
Slip of paper and pen
Food colouring, green works well but use a colour that you are drawn to
Clean jam jar with a lid

Gather your items together and sit in a quiet place. Take the slip of paper and pen and write an amount of money that you need. If you don't need a specific amount, write 'paid in full'. Pop the slip of paper into the bottom of the jar. Next hold the bowl of snow or ice in your hands and say:

"With the magic of transformation now
Ice or snow that melts, show me how
Money, prosperity and abundance for me
As the ice melts, money magic let me see"

Now tip the ice or snow into the jar, on top of the slip of paper. As it slides into the jar visualise money and prosperity coming your way and all your bills being paid off. Now add a few drops of food colouring. As you add the drops into the ice or snow say:

"Colour magic, money for me
Green is the colour for prosperity"

Put the lid on the jar and leave it somewhere safe, a windowsill works well, but bear in mind it may get slightly wet on the bottom! Allow the ice or snow to melt.

Leave it for three days to work its magic. Then you can tip the contents out onto the earth.

Crystal Money Magic Spell

To add energy to your crystal magic you can work a specific spell bringing in some candle magic to assist.

You will need:

A crystal (one from the list of suggestions above)
A candle in a safe holder, I like to use green, gold or orange for money magic
Bank statement, invoice or sheet of paper and a pen
Lighter/matches

Place your items in front of you and light the candle. Place the crystal in front of the candle and say:

"Crystal magic, stone to bring money in
Flame of candle, charge now to bring a win"

Take your bank statement or invoice, if you are using a piece of paper, you can write a sum of money on it that you need to bring in. Fold the paper/statement towards you to bring money in, then fold in the sides. Now take the crystal and place it on top of the folded paper. Say:

"Crystal magic, bring money to me
Crystal energy work quickly, so mote it be"

Place the paper and crystal on your altar or in a safe place until the spell has worked.

When the spell is done, the crystal can be cleansed for future use and the paper burnt or put in the trash.

Two Part Prosperity Animal Spell

This spell calls upon the energy of grasshopper to remove obstacles, make changes and bring abundance your way. Add to that the resourcefulness and saving abilities of squirrel and you have a nice neat money making and saving package.

You will need:

An image of a squirrel and a grasshopper, this can be a photo printed from the internet, a drawing or ornament
A black candle and a white candle in safe holders
Matches or a lighter
Two slips of paper
A pen or pencil
Cauldron or fireproof dish

Set the items out in front of you. Place the black candle in front of the grasshopper image and the white candle in front of the squirrel image.

Light the black candle. Take a slip of paper and write the words 'financial obstacles' on the paper. Light the slip of paper from the flame of the black candle and drop it into the cauldron. Now visualize any problems or obstacles that stand in the way of your finances, dissipating and being removed. Say:

"Power of grasshopper, financial restrictions and obstacles remove
With your magic my money and finances will improve"

Now light the white candle. Take a slip of paper and write the words 'improve my finances' on the paper. Light the slip of paper from the flame of the white candle and drop it into the cauldron. Now visualize money coming to you and financial opportunities opening up. Say:

Power of squirrel, with your money resources and helping me save
Open up opportunities for prosperity and abundance I crave

Sit quietly and focus on your goals and allow the candles to burn out. Keep the images of the squirrel and grasshopper somewhere prominent where you will see them regularly as a reminder.

Perfect Prosperity Pouch

Spell pouches are very simple to make but they pack a huge punch of magical power. You can make them personalized to you very easily. I have given the basic spell outline here but trust your intuition and what you feel guided to add. The pouch can be carried with you in your bag or popped your altar or bedside table.

You will need:

A small pouch, I use the coloured organza wedding favour bags, but you could use an old jewellery pouch, or a piece of fabric tied with a ribbon. If you like you can bring colour magic in and use a green, gold or silver bag to represent prosperity.

A green, gold or silver button
A small silver coin (such as a 5p piece)
Pinch of dried mint
Pinch of dried basil
Small piece of cinnamon stick
A whole nutmeg
A few grains of rice (dried, not cooked!)

Start by taking the pouch (or fabric) and holding it in your hands, visualize money, prosperity, abundance and new opportunities coming your way. Say:

"Prosperity pouch open up and hold abundance for me
With the ingredients I add to bring in prosperity"

Now you need to add each of the ingredients, charge them individually before you add them to the pouch visualizing prosperity coming your way each time. Hold the button in your hand and say:

"Button magic bring together abundance and prosperity for me"

Pop it in the bag. Hold the coin in your hand and say:

"Silver coin bring money magic to me"

Pop it in the bag. Hold the dried mint in your hand and say:

"Mint money come to me, with the addition of prosperity"

Pop it in the bag. Hold the dried basil in your hand and say:

"Basil magic bring abundance to me"

Pop it in the bag. Hold the piece of cinnamon stick in your hand and say:

> *"Cinnamon magic bring luck and success for me"*

Hold the nutmeg in your hand and say:

> *"Nutmeg bring luck and success to me"*

Pop it in the bag. Lastly take a few grains of rice in your hand, seven is a good magical number for money and say:

> *"Grains of rice added to bring money and abundance and keep it coming in"*

Once the bag is full of your items, tie the top and hold the bag in both hands and say:

> *"Prosperity pouch open up and hold abundance for me*
> *Full of ingredients now added to bring prosperity"*

If you feel the bag needs a boost of power give it a shake or add in a few extra pinches of dried mint or basil.

Money Magic Mug

What can be better on a cold day than a big steaming mug of hot chocolate? This warming comforting drink is an excellent vessel to carry magic, and it is very simple to do. Chocolate carries a huge punch of prosperity magic with it. Then adding in other ingredients boosts the abundance; peanuts, ginger, honey and nutmeg are all associated with prosperity and abundance.

You will need:

Half a pint of milk – any kind
Two squares of chocolate; plain, milk or white
For peanut hot chocolate add 1 tablespoon of peanut butter
For honey hot chocolate add 1 teaspoon honey
For spiced hot chocolate add a pinch of ground ginger and a pinch of ground nutmeg

Pop all the ingredients into a pan and gently heat, stirring until the chocolate squares have melted. Pour into your favourite mug. Hold the mug in your hands, close your eyes and visualise money and prosperity coming your way. Say:

"Chocolate that is hot and sweet
Bringing money to me would be neat
Chocolate that is sweet and hot
Money come to me and make it a lot"

Slowly sip your hot chocolate still visualising the abundance. When you are finished say:

"My gratitude and thanks on this day"

Abundance Hot Chocolate

This is a totally lush hot chocolate mix, make up larger quantities and keep the powder mix in a jar. It draws upon the magical energy of sugar to make life sweet, chocolate to draw prosperity in and cinnamon for success.

2 tablespoons Horlicks or a similar malted milk drink
2 tablespoons cornflour
3 tablespoons icing sugar
4 tablespoons cocoa powder

100g/3 ½ oz chocolate, finely grated (dark or milk)
1 pinch ground cinnamon
1 pinch salt

For an individual mug of hot chocolate with half a pint of milk use 5 heaped teaspoons of the mixture. Pour the milk into a saucepan and bring almost to the boil then spoon the chocolate mix into the hot milk, give it a whisk and leave to simmer in the saucepan for a couple of minutes before serving – it will come together as a nice thick gloopy consistency. Serve as is or top with whipped cream, marshmallows or a sprinkling of grated chocolate.

As you stir the ingredients in the pan make sure you stir the spoon clockwise, this will bring in positive energy and draw money to you. As you stir say:

"Sweet and sugary, chocolate fine
Bring prosperity in to make abundance mine"

Then as you drink the hot chocolate visualise money and prosperity coming your way.

Yule Tree Magic

Most of us will be putting up a tree to decorate. It doesn't matter if it is a real pine or spruce or an imitation one. The important aspect is that it is a Yule tree. Green is an excellent prosperity and money colour. With the abundance of needles on a pine tree it also corresponds nicely with bringing in money. Add in the money magic by decorating with baubles and tinsel that represent wealth. Green and gold are perfect colours, silver works too and red adds a bit of fiery power to it all.

You will need:

A Yule tree (any size)

Lights
Baubles
Tinsel or other decorations

Once your tree is set up add your lights. Then you are ready. I like to bless my tree first.

Stand in front of the tree and reach out your hand to touch the branches. Say:

"With the blessings of the year
Let's get this abundance magic into gear
Festive fun and joy about
Let's give prosperity a shout"

Now hold each ornament in your hands and visualise money and prosperity coming your way. You may even like to trace a pound or dollar sign with your finger into each item. As you hang each bauble, decoration or tinsel on the tree say:

"Decorations shiny and bright
Bring wealth and prosperity to light
Money and abundance come to me
With the power of the festive Yule tree"

Once your tree is fully decorated it should positively be singing with money magic energy.

Family Success Charm

With a lot of households getting together to celebrate not just Yule but also the arrival of the New Year I like to create a charm using the energy of the season to bring success for all the family members for the coming year. You can hang it up as a festive decoration on the tree and then once you take the decorations down you can hang it in a corner, I would suggest in the most central room of the house. It can then be renewed next Yule.

You will need:

A clear plastic bauble that opens up (you can get these in craft stores) or if you prefer, a square of brightly coloured fabric or felt (approx. 15cm square). I like to use yellow or orange as they are colours that represent happiness and success. If you use fabric, you will also need a piece of ribbon to tie it up.
A penny for luck
A holly leaf for success and protection
Three cloves for protection and money
A piece of cinnamon stick for success and love
A photograph of your family
A festive candle in a safe holder
Lighter or matches
Festive music

Lay your items out on a flat surface in front of you and switch on some uplifting festive music, this will help build the happy energy. Set the candle in front of you and light the flame. Take a moment to watch the flame as it burns and listen to the music, sing along if you want to raise extra positive energy. When you feel sufficiently jolly start to create your charm.

Open the bauble or piece of fabric. Place the photograph in the centre and visualise a happy, successful time for all your family members. Say:

"For each family member I dedicate this charm to ensure success
In wishes, hopes, desires and pure happiness"

Now place the penny on top of the photograph, visualise money and prosperity flowing to your family. Say:

"A lucky penny I place here
To bring prosperity and good fortune for the coming year"

Now add the holly leaf, still working with the visualisation and say:

"Power of holly to bring protection and success
To each member of my family for their happiness"

Next add in the cloves and say:

"Cloves I now add, to the power of three
To bring protection and abundance for my family and me"

Lastly add in the cinnamon stick and say:

"Cinnamon with the power of success and love
Bring this to my whole family from above"

Place the top of the bauble on and fix securely or bring the pieces of fabric together and tie with a ribbon. Take your charm in both hands and hold it up to the candlelight, keep visualising a year of success and happiness for your entire family. Say:

"Fire of the festive sun please bless now this charm
Fill our family with success and love so warm
A year of positive energy and success
For our home and family please now bless"

Allow the candle to burn down and sit listening to the music and visualising all the good positive energy for the year ahead. Then hang the charm on your Yule tree.

Tree Blessing

Most of us will have a tree at Yule decked out with lights and sparkles. Before you decorate your tree how about giving it a blessing to bring abundance, prosperity and positive energy in? It doesn't matter if it is a real or fake one, the blessing works just the same. If you have green garlands and wreaths for decoration these can be blessed to.

You will need:

A dish of water
Salt
Festive incense or a scented candle
Lighter or matches

Work this magic once your tree is set in place but before you decorate it. Light your incense or scented candle. Stand in front of your tree and walk around it clockwise. Walking clockwise brings in positive energy. You are going to walk around the tree three times.

As you walk waft the smoke from the incense or the scent from the candle with one hand, towards the tree.

On the first circle say *"I give blessings to this tree, that it may be a sign of great positivity"*

On the second round say *"With the element of fire, I request all that I desire"*

On the third round say *"With my blessings to this tree, may it bring abundance and success to me"*

Now put the candle or incense down in a safe place to burn out. Take your dish of water and add a pinch of salt, stir it with your finger clockwise. Stand in front of your tree and walk around it clockwise. You are going to walk around the tree three times again. As you walk dip your fingers into the salt water and flick it onto the tree. (Just lightly, you don't want to soak the tree!).

On the first circle say *"I give blessings to this tree, that it may be a sign of great positivity"*

On the second circle say *"Water is my blessing to thee, to bring abundance and prosperity"*

On the third circle say *"Salt of earth and power of life, to keep away stress and strife"*

Now stand in front of the tree and say:

"Blessings to my festive tree
To bring abundance and prosperity
With love and light and power to me
My thanks and gratitude to thee"

Sunset Releasing Spell

Either sit outside so that you can see the sunset or get in a position where you can see it through your window. This spell will help release any debts or financial worries you have.

You will need:

Four candles – colours of your choice but I suggest tying them in with the colours of a sunset (yellow, orange, pink and red). If you don't have coloured candles, white will be fine.

Four slips of paper and a pen
Fireproof dish

Light all four candles. Write down on each slip of paper what it is you would like to let go of, whether it is an overdraft, outstanding bills or credit card debts. It only needs to be a word or two. Set fire to a slip of paper from the first candle and pop it in the fireproof dish to burn. Take another slip of paper and set fire to it from the second candle and pop it in the dish to burn.

Repeat with the third and fourth candle. Say a chant each time:

"With the setting of the sun
Releasing my debts is now down"

Then snuff out the candles in reverse order. Finally look towards the sun as it sets below the horizon and say out loud

"The end of my woes, ready for the beginning of a new day"

Sunrise Fresh Start Spell

Using the sunset spell as a template, you can work the spell as the sun begins to rise at the beginning of the day, using the intent for new beginnings and a new start for your financial situation.

You will need:

Four candles – colours of your choice but I suggest tying them in with the colours of a sunrise (pale yellow, white, baby pink and pale blue). If you don't have coloured candles, white will be fine.

Four slips of paper and a pen
Fireproof dish

Light all four candles. Write down on each slip of paper what it is you would like to start, a new project, a fresh beginning or an increase in your money. It only needs to be a word or two.

Set fire to a slip of paper from the first candle and pop it in the fireproof dish to burn. Take another slip of paper and set fire to it from the second candle and pop it in the dish to burn. Repeat with the third and fourth candle. Say a chant each time:

"With the rising of the sun
Abundance and wealth my way will come"

Then snuff out the candles in reverse order. Finally look towards the sun as it rises and say out loud:

"As the sun begins to rise, abundance and fresh starts I surmise"

Goal Sun Tarot Spell

You will need:

Sun tarot card or an image of one printed off the net
A slip of paper
Pen or pencil
Crystal you associate with the sun and abundance, citrine would work well

Using the Sun tarot card and picking a crystal of your choice. Write your goal on a slip of paper, be specific, it might be that you want to get a new job, bring in more money, find some extra cash fast or just get your finances sorted. Lay the paper slip on your altar (or somewhere that it won't be disturbed). Take the Sun tarot card and say out loud your request, holding the card in front of you. Add a chant such as:

"Tarot magic, power of the sun
Debts and poverty now be gone
Abundance and prosperity come to me
Sun magic bring these for me to see"

Place the tarot card on top of your slip of paper. Charge the crystal in your hand with the same desire, repeating the chant and pop that on top of the tarot card. Leave it in place for seven days, re-charging the crystal and re-energising the spell by saying your desire out loud at least once a day. On the seventh day burn or bury the slip of paper and cleanse the card and crystal for re-use.

To add extra solar power, you could start this spell on a Sunday. Let the sun do its thing.

Solar Candle Spell

This is a multi-purpose spell that can be used for any intent that corresponds to solar energy. I like to use it for fast money or abundance.

You will need:

A candle – colour of your choice, but green, gold or orange work well for money, wealth and success
A crystal of your choice, I like to work with green aventurine or citrine for abundance and money
Herbs to correspond, so dried mint or basil work well

Set your candle outside in the sunshine in a safe place on a fireproof dish. Hold the crystal in your hand and charge it with your intent and pop it in front of the candle. Charge the herbs with your intent and sprinkle them around the candle. Light the candle and sit quietly visualising your desires and goals. See them happening in your mind's eye, visualise the debts disappearing and the money rolling in. Ask the sun to lend its energy to the spell. Say the chant:

"Draw the power of the sun
Debts and bills are now gone
Abundance, prosperity and money now
Solar magic show me how"

Sit with the candle until it burns out. Sprinkle the herbs on the ground and carry the crystal with you. To add power to your spell time it with the sun's position in the sky; sunrise for new projects and beginnings and for bringing money to you, midday for power and strength and sunset to release any debts.

Sun Candles

December marks the winter solstice, when we celebrate the return of the sun and the longer days of sunlight. The sun is very powerful and can help boost any kind of magic. Working with candlelight can bring prosperity and abundance your way and add to the festive decorations.

You will need:

One large candle
Several smaller candles, 6 or 9 would work well
Greenery such as holly which brings luck and success and ivy and pine for abundance
Coloured ribbons

Choose colours for your candles and ribbons that you associate with wealth and money such as gold and green.
Candle holders
Pine or cinnamon essential oil (optional)

Create a centre piece for your dining room table (or your mantelpiece). If you wish you can dress the candles with essential oil, pine for prosperity or cinnamon for success would work well. Dressing the candle means brushing the oil onto the outside surfaces of the candle. You don't need to do this step, but it all adds to the magic.

Set the large candle in the centre in a safe holder, put the other candles around it, again in safe holders. Entwine the greenery and ribbons around the candles, making sure none of it is anywhere near the top of the candle where the flame will be. As you put your creation together try visualising money and abundance coming your way.

If you aren't creative, you could purchase readymade garlands or wreaths which can be set in and around the candles.

When your sun candle decoration is ready you can start the spell; if you are able to work it on a waxing or full moon that will add to the power as well, as both these phases will help bring money to you. Light the central candle and say:

"As we celebrate the return of the sun
Abundance, prosperity and money to come
Bringing light and warmth back now to us
Power of the sun deliver here with no fuss"

Now light each candle in turn and repeat the same chant for each one. Once all your candles are all alight say:

"With the power of the sunshine
Wealth and money will be mine"

Allow the candles to burn whilst you sit and visualise your home being filled with an abundance of happiness and good cheer. And see your finances growing with ease. When you are ready snuff out the candles. These can be lit again during the festive period for decoration but please don't leave them unattended.

Winter Solstice Savings Spell

As the winter solstice celebrates the returning of the sun, and the days that follow bring more sunlight each day we can work with that energy to increase your finances. As it is the festive season it makes sense to add a little glitter to boost the magic, and who doesn't love glitter?

You will need:

- A yellow or gold candle
- A candle holder
- Matches or lighter
- Oil – this can be plain olive or sunflower oil from the kitchen
- Glitter
- A knife or skewer

First you need to prepare the candle. Take your knife or skewer and carve a pound sign into the side of the candle wax. It doesn't need to be perfect; it just needs to be a nod to money. As you carve say:

"Winter solstice candle I imbue
Money and prosperity into you"

Next using your fingers or a small brush cover the candle with a light film of oil. Brush the oil from the base of the candle upwards to the top, to show that you are bringing positive energy into the spell. Then sprinkle glitter all over the candle, this is easier if you first sprinkle the glitter onto a chopping board first and then roll the candle in it. As you do so say:

"Glitter, sparkle and shine
Money, prosperity and abundance be mine"

Now set your candle in a safe holder.

You will need to wash your hands at this point!

Light the wick and sit quietly watching the flame, visualise being able to save money, bit by bit, gradually adding to your savings and building up a nice sum. Say:

"Winter solstice and return of the sun
Build on my finances one by one
Boost my money, add to the pot
Allow me to save and make it a lot"

When you are ready you can snuff the candle out. I would suggest repeating this process over a period of 8 days, 8 is the number of wealth and achievement. It will only take a few minutes each day, but you will be adding to the solstice energy by building up your magic each day. Once you have finished you can dispose of the candle stub.

Remember you will need to back this up in the real world by making an effort to save.

Positive Prosperity

A lot of us will be decorating our homes for the festive season. And you can add some money making, prosperous magic into every item you decorate with. You can also boost that abundance energy by singing carols, yep you heard me correctly!

You will need:

Any kind of decorations, whether you are putting up a tree or decorating the table or the rest of the house
Christmas carol music
Duster or cleaning cloth
Spray bottle filled with distilled water
A few drops of pine essential oil or a sprig of pine tree
You can get spray/spritz bottles from the pound stores.

To make distilled water, boil a kettle of water and allow it to cool then fill a spray bottle with it. The boiled and cooled water creates distilled water which helps to keep the water fresh.

Add a few (for an average size spray bottle add about 5 drops of essential oil) drops of oil to the water in the bottle. If you have a sprig of pine tree that can be dropped into the bottle. Close the lid and give it a shake. As you shake it say:

"Essence of prosperity making pine
Season's greetings to make life fine
As I spread magic and song
Bring in abundance and don't take long"

Now put on some Christmas carols, this will help you get into the festive mood, but also raises the positive energy. If you know the words sing along, this also helps to boost the energy as you decorate. You want to raise the vibrations in your home as high as you can!

With each decoration you put out, whether it is a bauble, tinsel or a hanging decoration, spray a little of the pine water onto your cleaning cloth and give the item a wipe. As you do so say:

"Christmas energy to fill this home
Prosperity, abundance and then some

Festive cheer to bring in money and love
Along with all the positive things we think of!"

Keep going with each item until your home is full of festive decorations, song and positive abundance filled energy.

Scented Simmering Pot

A huge part of getting into the festive mood for me are the scents that we associate with this time of the year. Cinnamon, nutmeg, cloves and orange for example. All of them together just bring up childhood memories of fabulous Yule times. Each of these spices are packed with magical properties and a lot of them work well for prosperity and success magic.

This is an idea to fill your house with the scent of the season whilst working some powerful money magic at the same time. You don't need to limit this to December, you can create money magic simmering pots at any time of the year.

You will need:

A saucepan half filled with water
Two cinnamon sticks – for success and positive changes
Half a nutmeg (grated) – for money and luck
9 cloves – for money
1 orange, sliced – for generosity, energy and happiness
3 slices of root ginger or a teaspoon of ground ginger – for success and prosperity
1 star anise – for good luck

You can use all or some of the above ingredients, experiment and see which scents you prefer. Pop the ingredients into the pan of water and put on a low heat. Stir clockwise and say:

"Spices filled with money magic power
Prosperity, abundance and success on me will shower"

Leave the pan on a low simmer until it fills the house with a beautiful festive scent. Keep an eye on it to make sure it doesn't boil dry. You can top up the water if necessary.

Once you are finished the water can be poured onto the earth as an offering.

Yuletide Spice Spell

This spell uses some of the familiar festive spices to not only bring about money and prosperity but also a happy home. With the added bonus that it makes the house smell amazing.

You will need:

A saucepan
Water
Wooden spoon
One cinnamon stick or a heaped teaspoon of ground cinnamon
A piece of root ginger or a heaped teaspoon of ground ginger
An orange, sliced
A teaspoon of ground nutmeg
Three star anise

Fill your saucepan half full with water. Break the cinnamon stick in half and pop it in the water or add the ground cinnamon. Stir the pan three times in a clockwise direction and say:

"Cinnamon spice and all things nice

Now I stir the water around thrice
Bring success and money my way
Money and success come this day"

Next take the root ginger and slice it or use ground ginger, add it to the pan. Stir the pan three times in a clockwise direction and say:

"Ginger spice and all things nice
Now I stir the water around thrice
Success and prosperity come my way
Bring these things now within this day"

Add the slices of orange to the pan. Stir the water three times in a clockwise direction and say:

"Orange slices and all things nice
Now I stir the water around thrice
Generosity may come my way
I will also give generosity this day"

Add the ground nutmeg to the pan. Stir the water three times in a clockwise direction and say:

"Nutmeg spice and all things nice
Now I stir the water around thrice
Luck and money will come my way
Bring prosperity to me this day"

Now heat the pan on a low temperature. It needs to simmer until the scent of the ingredients fill the air throughout your home. You can keep it on a very low heat for an hour or two to really get the full effect.

Once you are done, put the ingredients into your compost bin or trash and pour the water onto the soil in your garden if possible.

Pinecone Prosperity Decorations

Pine brings with it a strong magical protection for your home and also a sense of hospitality and welcome. Keeping pine needles or cones in your home brings in abundance. The Yule tree is obviously pine and so it brings a huge punch of wealth and prosperity with it. Pinecones can easily be found at this time of the year and make very pretty decorations but can also have some money magic added to them.

What you need:

Pinecones (obviously!)
Equal amounts cinnamon, nutmeg and allspice, mixed together
A 1:1 mixture of water and craft glue
Glitter – gold and green are colours associated with money and wealth
Ribbon
A small paintbrush
Baking sheet

- Run the pinecones under water for a few seconds then spread them out on a baking sheet. Bake in the oven at 200C/400F/Gas 6 for about 20 minutes. The baking process makes the pinecones open up and also destroys any bacteria that might be lurking on them. If you obtained your pinecones from a craft shop you will be able to skip this step.
- Cool the pinecones and then apply the glue mix. It is up to you whether you coat the entire pinecone with glue, just the odd petal or just the tips – be creative!

- Mix together the spices and the glitter, the spices all bring the magic of success and prosperity. Then shake the mix onto the pinecones or alternatively (and probably the least messy option) put the spice/glitter mix into a plastic bag then drop the pinecone in and give it a shake.

Once the glue on the pinecones is dry, pop a few of them in a pretty dish to display or you can tie a piece of ribbon around each one and use them to hang on your Yule tree.

Sigil Money Magic

Sigils are a personal way of drawing a magical symbol and will be unique to you and each one will be different depending on what you want to bring in.

You will need:

A piece of paper
A pen

First you need an intent and a phrase that sums up your intended outcome. It might be 'I am prosperous and successful' or 'I am financially stable and debt free'. Keep it positive and simple.

I like to work with "draw money to me". We will use the letters of the phrase to create the sigil, but we need to simplify it first by removing all the vowels and any letters that are duplicated, once you have done that you end up with:

"drwmnyt"

Now you need to grab a pen and paper and draw the letters, you can draw them one on top of another or you can space them out linking them together – be guided by your intuition and be as creative or as simple as you want. Create a pleasing image using the letters.

Once you have done that your sigil is complete. Your intent is in the letters, so you can bury it in the earth, burn it in the fire or wash it away in water – whatever works for you. This will release the energy into the Universe and kick start the sigil magic.

Magic Circle

This spell uses the letters of the alphabet and a statement as we used in the sigil. This time we add in the magic of a circle. Circles have their own magical energy and, in this case, can work as a continuous never-ending cycle of magic to keep the money rolling in.

You will need:

A piece of paper
A pen

- Start by writing out your request, let's use the same one as before 'draw money to me'. You can use the phrase complete, or you can remove the vowels and any duplicated letters.
- So, you would end up with "drwmnyt".
- Now you need to draw a circle on the paper, I find it easier to trace around the base of a glass or cup.
- Next write the alphabet around the inside edge of the circle.
- Now draw a line connecting the first letter of your shortened phrase to the second letter. So, you would draw a line from 'd' to 'r', then draw a line from the 'r' to the 'w' and continue until you have connected all the letters.
- What you have now created is a money draw sigil.

- You may like to say a chant to kick start the magic, say:
- "Never ending energy, magic of the circle round
- Bring prosperity and money to me, this magic is now bound"
- You can burn the paper, bury it in the earth or wash it away to release the energy. Or you could draw the shape of the sigil on the inside of your purse or wallet to keep the money flowing it.

Witch Tips

Be specific about what you want to attract, be prepared to follow the spell up with practical action but most of all...believe in yourself and that you are deserving.

Keep some of the pine needles from your Yule tree. Pop a few in your purse and some under your front door mat. Pine symbolizes money and prosperity and helps keep the money coming in.

Drill holes in whole nutmegs and nuts such as pecans and string them on ribbon to hang on the Yule tree. It will look fabulous but also bring prosperity magic in.

Don't have tarot or oracle cards? Playing cards can be used instead. The diamonds suit represents money and finances. 10 of Diamonds represents prosperity and good fortune and 9 of diamonds is new opportunities and unexpected money.

Add a pinch of chilli powder to your spell workings, it carries a huge boost of energy and will help your spell to work faster.

Trace the number 6 or 8 on your bank card with your finger before you put it in your wallet to keep money coming in.

Trace your favourite prosperity symbol onto your debit or credit card with your finger before you place it into your purse or wallet, to help money stay in your account.

Burn it! If you have debts and unpaid bills, take a copy of them so that you can actually pay them, but burning the invoice/bill can help send a message to the universe that you need help to reduce the debt. Throw it in the fire or set light to it and drop it in a safe fireproof container.

When you decorate your tree, get each family member to write a wish on a piece of ribbon and tie it to the Yule tree.

Write the word 'money' on a small leaf and keep it in your purse to bring prosperity your way.

Drop a peppermint tea bag into a bucket of hot water and use it to wash your floors and windowsills, as you go visualise money coming into your home.

Glitter makes everything sparkle, if you have some charge it with positive prosperity energy and sprinkle a pinch into your purse to help boost the money coming in.

Try plaiting three pieces of cord together with the intent of prosperity, wear it as a bracelet or tie it to your car/house key chain.

Both rice and oats bring the magical energy of fertility, for new beginnings, prosperity, money or any new opportunities. You can eat both of them with those goals in mind.

Stand in your shower each morning and visualise the water washing away negative energy and leaving you positive charged to receive prosperity and abundance.

Sprinkle your cash with a pinch of baking powder to help your money grow or add some to your spells to increase the power.

Be aware of any animals that you see when you are out and about, whether you see one in the park, on TV or in a magazine. It might be a message that money is coming to you!

Words have power, if you want to create your own chants but aren't too good with rhyming words you can do a Google search for 'rhyming dictionary' – it really helps.

Coffee is a fire element ingredient, each morning when you drink your coffee visualise having a prosperous day with each sip.

Look out for repeating numbers in your daily life, do you keep seeing the same number all the time? It may have an important meaning and hopefully a prosperous one!

Place a dish containing sand or small seeds on a table in your home. Add in a handful of mixed tumble stones. When you feel the need, pick up one of the crystals and make a wish, then make a pattern with the crystals inside the dish with your wish stone at the centre.

If you need a quick money spell sing a chant to yourself. Quietly under your breath or out loud. Something simple like *"money, money, money, come to me, money, money, money let it be"*.

Add an extra boost of magic to your money magic by writing your sigils or petitions in a green or gold pen. Green for prosperity and gold for abundance.

The sun brings a powerful boost of manifesting energy. Write your request for money on a slip of paper and leave it out in the sunshine.

Left over chocolate? In the unlikely event that you do, utilise the chocolate by melting it in a mug of hot milk and sprinkling in a pinch of cinnamon. The chocolate brings prosperity and cinnamon gives a boost of success. As you sip you could chant:

"magic chocolate, delicious and lush,
bring good things to me in a rush"

If you want to boost the energy to a spell you could add in a pinch of ground ginger, mustard powder, black pepper, cinnamon, cloves, coriander, cumin, garlic, nutmeg, rosemary or even a bit of tobacco. All these spices are full of fire power and will add a magical oomph to the spell.

Boost your magical workings by using colour magic. Each colour is associated with magical intent.

All flowers and plants have magical properties, some of them are particularly good for prosperity and abundance. Especially during the summer months when they are all in full bloom. These are particularly good: Basil, chamomile, clover, cornflower, dandelion, heather, holly, honeysuckle, ivy, jasmine, marigold, mint, nettle, pine, poppy, rose, sage or sunflower.

Pop a leaf or a petal in your purse, grow them in your garden or keep a vase of cut flowers in your home to keep the money and abundance flowing.

If you have a bill or invoice that you don't have the money for just at the moment, fold it up and pop it in the freezer. This will put the matter on hold for a while. Only for a while though, you will need to deal with it at some point!

Coins carry their own magic, particularly silver and gold ones. Keep a silver or gold coin in your purse or wallet at all times, never leave it completely empty. It will help keep the money flowing.

When you bake bread, cookies or pastry carve a symbol into the dough. It might be a pound or dollar sign, something that symbolises money and abundance to you. Most doughs include flour of some kind which brings the magic of abundance anyway, but by baking a symbol in you get added magical power.

Days of the week have particular magical correspondences. For money and prosperity spells work them on a Wednesday, Thursday or Sunday for the best results. To bring success for a project work your spell on a Tuesday. For a change in luck work your spell on a Wednesday.

Corn carries the magical properties of abundance and prosperity (the colour yellow is positive and the fact that the cobs have lots of kernels represents abundance). You can work prosperity magic by making popcorn. Pop the kernels in a pan with melted butter or oil (which also carries the energy of wealth), sprinkle them with sugar (to make life sweet) and eat your way to prosperity.

If a leaf is big enough it can be used to write wishes and petitions on that can be sent away on the winds, buried in the earth, dropped into running water or burnt in the fire. If you don't want to write on a leaf or you are out and about and don't have a pen with you, select a leaf and hold it in both hands then lift it up to your face and whisper your wish into it, fold it over and then allow the wind to take it away.

Chestnuts are a big part of the festive scene. They bring with them the magic of success, abundance and prosperity. Eat them roasted or pop a bowl of chestnuts in your home to bring the magic in.

Pop a silver coin into the bottom of your plant pot before you put the seeds or plants in. Give it a little blessing to grow your bank account as the seeds and plants grow.

Open the windows. I know it seems simple but let in the fresh air. Allow it to cleanse and clear out any negative energy from your home. As you open the window ask the wind to bring prosperity and abundance.

Wash your doorstep with the herbal water to help bring abundance into the house.

If you use a number or letter combination to unlock your phone screen, how about using a word that works with prosperity to unlock it? You the word 'money' perhaps?

If you are lucky enough to see a rainbow, then make a wish. You don't need to find the pot of gold at the end, just look up to the sky and take in the gorgeous colours that Mother Nature creates and ask for your desire.

The leaves from some plants are particularly associated with luck and abundance. Work with ivy leaves for success, maple leaves for abundance and oak for prosperity.

Bring some blossoms and greenery into your home to symbolize the fertility of the season, new beginnings and a flush of luck.

Set out a dish or jar of water first thing in the morning and allow it to soak up the energy from the sun throughout the day. Take it in at sunset. This water can be used to dab onto money to increase your wealth.

Cinnamon brings the magic of success, add a pinch to your hot beverage to give your money-making magic a successful outcome.

Use green embroidery thread or wool and place knots in it and tie it around your wrist to carry a reminder of money magic with you.

Keep a pot of herbs on your kitchen windowsill to bring in the money, basil and mint are both really good prosperity herbs to have.

If you find a coin and it is laying heads up then it is considered to be a lucky coin, pick it up and use it in money drawing and prosperity spells. If you spot a coin and it is laying tails up then don't take it, it is considered to bring bad luck you should however turn the coin over so that the next person to find it will have good luck.

Save the seeds when you carve your pumpkins, pumpkin seeds not only make a yummy snack they also work brilliantly in prosperity magic. Bake pumpkin into pies and casseroles to bring abundance and money to your life.

You don't need to use the actual nuts for magical spells. Eat the nuts to take on the prosperity magic but save the shells. The shells can then be used for your spell work.

Lots of leaves and seeds carry the magic of prosperity and can be popped into your purse or bag to keep money coming in. Try hazel leaves, beech leaves, basil leaves, mint leaves, cloves, fenugreek seeds, mint leaves, oak leaves, rose petals, a star anise or poppy seeds.

Place a small change money jar or dish by your front door or just inside your hallway. Add a few coins to it regularly. Not only will you actually be accruing money, you will be sending out magical energy to bring money into your home.

Solar Divination can give you some answers or guidance. Stand outside when the sun is shining, somewhere that you can see shadows. Ask for help with your finances and watch the rays of sun and where the shadows fall and move to see any images or shapes that give you an answer.

Don't forget you can also boost the money magic of the hot coals by adding herbs to burn. Sage is excellent for clearing debts but also brings in abundance and carries the magic of wishes. Basil and mint are both excellent herbs for wealth, money and prosperity, just add a pinch of each on top of the hot coals.

Collect pinecones when you are out and about. Pine brings the magic of prosperity, money and abundance. Keep them in a bowl just inside your doorway to bring money into the house.

Charge your hand moisturiser with prosperity magic as you apply it. Squeeze out the amount you need into the palm of your hand and use one of the prosperity chants from above as you rub it into your hands. The same can be done with our body moisturiser.

When you have finished with your carved pumpkin, write a wish on a slip of paper and pop it into the pumpkin, then bury the pumpkin in the garden.

Stir a spoonful of honey or sugar into your hot beverage to 'make life sweet'.

Write the word 'money' or 'prosperity' inside your purse of wallet with a Sharpie pen to activate the money word magic.

Trace the shape of the infinity sign on any cash before you put it in your wallet, to symbolize a continuous stream of money.

Rose petals are edible, pop a couple into your cup of tea charging them with abundance and luck energy.

Folklore says that a garment with eight buttons on is lucky. Also having a garment with an odd number of buttons brings in luck too.

Make sure your toilet seat is put back in the down position. Leaving the toilet lid up can cause household money to drain away!

Types of Spells

There are all different types of spells you can work with to bring prosperity, abundance and money into your life. All of the suggested spells and correspondences in this book can be adapted to work with most types of spell. Here are my suggestions:

Candle Magic – My advice would be to work with small spell candles or even birthday cake candles as they burn quickly. However, tea lights and small votives also work well if you have time to watch them. Dinner/taper candles work well if you are spreading the magic over a few days so you can light the wick, burn it for a short while, snuff it out and then relight it. Pillar candles I reserve for use on my altar and don't usually use in spell working as they take so long to burn. Candle magic means you can bring in colour magic in the form of the candle, you can also dress the candle with essential oil and roll in dried herbs to add more layers. Candles can also have symbols and sigils carved into them.

Spell Pouch – Spell pouches can be created from pieces of fabric or felt tied with twine or ribbon. Organza bags work well as they come in a variety of colours, although they don't hold fine powdered herbs very well! You can even use envelopes or pieces of folded paper; these work well if you have an envelope that a bill or bank statement came in as it holds the magic of money already.

Magic Powder – These can be created by grinding up herbs and spices and used to 'feed' or recharge your spell pouches.

Witch Ladders and Knot Magic – I have included a couple of spells using ladders, knots and plaiting these all work well to bind the magic into the cords.

Jar Spells and Witch Bottles – I use jars a lot as they provide useful containers to fill with your spell ingredients. Try using jars that have held prosperity ingredients such as mint sauce or peanut butter. You can even create container spells using cardboard packets or tin cans.

Petition Papers – These are slips of paper that you write your intent on in short form, just a word or two to state your goal. These papers are then added to your spell working, often they are burnt to set the magic in motion. Bring in colour magic by using coloured paper and coloured ink.

Correspondences

There are certain crystals, herbs, foods and plants that correspond to drawing money, prosperity and abundance. This is not set in stone, use your intuition and be guided by what resonates with you, but these lists may give you a starting point. Add these into your spell working to add an extra layer of prosperity magic.

Crystals

These can be charged with your intent and placed on your altar, carried with you or popped around your home. Place them in front of candle spells to add to the energy or add them to spell pouches, witch bottles or jar spells.

Attraction – Copper, garnet

Beginnings – Moss agate, kyanite, malachite, moonstone, rhodochrosite

Business matters – Amethyst, malachite

Changes – Amethyst, calcite (orange), citrine, labradorite, lepidolite, malachite, rhodonite

Fertility – Moss agate, jade (nephrite), moonstone, pebble/hag stone, quartz (rose)

Finances – Moss agate, calcite (orange), hematite, jade (nephrite), malachite, pyrite, turquoise

Growth – Moss agate, kyanite, malachite, pyrite, quartz (rose), unakite

Happiness – Blue lace agate, moss agate, amethyst, aventurine (green), celestite, chrysoprase, citrine, gold, jasper, larimar, lepidolite, quartz (rose), rhodochrosite, rhodonite, sunstone, tourmaline, unakite

Luck – Moss agate, amethyst, aventurine (green), carnelian, chrysoprase, copper, goldstone, jade (nephrite), kyanite, labradorite, lapis lazuli, lepidolite, obsidian (black), petrified wood, pyrite, quartz (rose), quartz (smoky), sunstone, tiger's eye, turquoise

Manifesting – Amber, fluorite, goldstone, hematite, jade (nephrite), jade (nephrite), lapis lazuli, malachite, pebble, pyrite, quartz, quartz (smoky), rhodochrosite, serpentine, silver

Money – Aventurine (green), bloodstone, calcite (orange), copper, goldstone, hematite, malachite, selenite, tiger's eye

Opportunities – Aventurine (green), calcite (orange), carnelian, lepidolite, malachite, sunstone, tiger's eye

Prosperity – Blue lace agate, moss agate, chrysoprase, gold, jade (nephrite), jasper, malachite, moonstone, pyrite, quartz (rose), quartz (smoky), rhodochrosite, serpentine, silver, sunstone, tiger's eye, turquoise

Releasing – Moss agate, calcite (orange), chrysocolla, chrysoprase, fluorite, howlite, jasper, lepidolite, malachite, obsidian (black), pyrite, quartz (smoky), rhodochrosite, rhodonite, sodalite, sugilite, tiger's eye, tourmaline, unakite

Stability – Moss agate, brass, carnelian, fluorite, hematite, jasper, kyanite, petrified wood, selenite, silver, sunstone, tourmaline, unakite

Success – Blue lace agate, moss agate, amber, amethyst, carnelian, chrysoprase, citrine, garnet, goldstone, labradorite, lapis lazuli, malachite, obsidian (black), petrified wood, pyrite, quartz (rose), selenite, serpentine, tiger's eye, unakite

Transformation – Amethyst, chrysoprase, gold, jasper (red/brick), kyanite, labradorite, lepidolite, malachite, petrified wood, tourmaline, unakite

Wealth – Moss agate, bloodstone, brass, calcite (orange), citrine, gold, jade (nephrite), lapis lazuli, malachite, moonstone, obsidian (black), pyrite, silver, tiger's eye, turquoise, unakite

Wishes – Amber, moonstone, quartz (smoky)

Herbs and Plants

Oil blends can be used to dress candles, herbs can be added to candles for spell work, popped into spell pouches, witch bottles or jar spells. Herbs and spices can be used to create incense blends or spell powders.

Abundance – Bergamot, Buttercup, Camellia, Clove, Cornflower (Batchelor's Buttons), Cumin, Dandelion, Echinacea, Frankincense, Grass, Heliotrope, Horseradish, Hyacinth, Ivy, Orchid, Pine, Rose, Sage, Saint John's Wort

Beginnings – Birch, crocus

Business – Pennyroyal

Changes – Cinnamon, primrose

Fertility – Birch, Bracken, Catnip, Chickweed, Cornflower (Batchelor's Buttons), Cyclamen, Daffodil, Dock, Fennel,

Geranium, Hawthorn, Hazel, Horsetail, Mistletoe, Mustard, Oak, Parsley, Pine, Poppy, Sunflower, Walnut

Growth – Primrose

Happiness – African violet, Agrimony, Basil, Borage, Catnip, Celandine, Crocus, Cyclamen, Daisy, Dragon's Blood, Hawthorn, Hyacinth, Lavender, Lily of the Valley, Marigold, Marjoram, Meadowsweet, Parsley, Peony, Saint John's Wort, Sunflower, Sweetpea, Yarrow

Luck – Agrimony, Aloe, Angelica, Beech, Broom, Calamus, Clover, Daffodil, Elm, Hazel, Heather, Holly, Horseradish, Marigold, Nutmeg, Oak, Peony, Poppy, Rose, Star Anise, Sunflower

Money – Basil, Bergamot (orange), Bladder wrack, Calamus, Cedar, Chamomile, Clove, Clover, Comfrey, Dill, Dock, Fenugreek, Flax, Ginger, Goldenrod, Gorse, Honesty, Jasmine, Mint, Myrtle, Nettle, Nutmeg, Oak, Patchouli, Periwinkle, Poppy, Vervain, Woodruff

Prosperity – Ash, Basil, Benzoin, Camellia, Fenugreek, Hazel, Honeysuckle, Mandrake, Patchouli, Scullcap, Tulip

Releasing – Alexanders, Birch, Carnation, Celandine, Coriander, Cypress, Lungwort, Self Heal, Thyme, Willow

Success – Beech, Bergamot (orange), Cinnamon, Clover, Cumin, Ginger, Holly, Lemon Balm, Lily of the Valley, Rowan, Sage, Solomon's Seal

Transformation – Yew

Wealth – Basil, coriander

Wishes – Beech, Dandelion, Hazel, Sage, Sandalwood (white), Sunflower, Sweetgrass, Walnut, Willow

Foods

These can be eaten to impart prosperity magic or used in spell workings.

Beginnings – Cherry, eggs, lamb, pomegranate

Fertility – Avocado, beef, blackberry, blueberry, cabbage, carrot, cherry, chestnut, chicken, corn, cucumber, eggs, elderflower, figs, fish, grapes, hazelnut, lamb, lettuce, mango, oats, olives, onions, parsley, peach, pomegranate, pork, rice, soya, spinach, strawberry, sunflower seed, walnut, watercress

Growth – Artichoke, sunflower, pomegranate

Happiness – Basil, cake, lavender, cheese, chocolate, grapefruit, honey, jelly, lemon, lemongrass, marjoram, orange, parsley, pine nut, quince, radish, saffron, sunflower seed, wine

Luck – Chicken, corn, kumquat, nutmeg, olives, pear, pineapple, poppy seeds, pork, soya, star anise, strawberry

Prosperity/Money/Wealth/Abundance – Almond, apple, aubergine, banana, basil, bean, bergamot, blackberry, Brazil nut, cabbage, cashew, chamomile, chestnut, chicken, chocolate, clove, clover, coriander, corn, cumin, elderflower, fish, ginger, honey, jasmine, kumquat, macadamia, maple syrup, mint, nasturtium, nutmeg, oats, peanut, pear, pecan, pineapple, poppy seeds, pork, potato, pumpkin, rice, sage, sesame, soya, sunflower seed, tea, wheat

Success – Bergamot, borage, cheese, chestnut, cinnamon, cumin, ginger, mustard, sage, strawberry

Wishes – Peach, pomegranate, sage, walnut, wheat

Colours

Each of us will have our own individual colours we associate with money and prosperity, these can be brought in with the colour of candles, altar clothes or ink, my suggestions are:

Green is for luck, prosperity, abundance and money magic
Orange is for attracting things, luck, selling and success
Purple is for business and ambition
Red is for strength, power and energy
Yellow is for prosperity and self-promotion
Gold is for abundance and wealth

Symbols

These can be carved into candles or drawn on petition papers:

Pound sign – perhaps the most obvious, it represents money, cash and keeping it rolling in.
Dollar or Euro sign – other familiar ones that are all about cold hard cash.
Numbers – if you need a specific amount of money, use numbers to represent the amount you need.
Infinity – this figure 8 on its side creates never ending energy
Zodiac signs – these represent prosperity and abundance – Taurus, Virgo, Cancer, Leo
Four leaf clover – bringing luck your way
Runes – Fehu, Gebo, Wunjo, Jera, Dagaz, Othila
Ogham – Duir/Oak, Quert/Apple, Edhadh/Aspen, Onn/Gorse, Muinn/Bramble, Gort/Ivy

Numbers

Use numbers in your spell work by chanting a certain number of times or using a particular number of ingredients.

No. 0 – The beginning that brings potential and new opportunities.

No. 1 – This is the connection to the universe, the life force that holds everything bound, it is the energy that ties us all together. Number one is the source. It is a grounding number that also brings personal power and control. It is a good number to work with for keeping your finances secure.

No. 2 – A number of balance and duality. Number two is all about opposites that attract such as light and dark. Being a dual number, it also covers partnerships of all kinds and relationships. A good number to use in business ventures.

No. 3 – Action! Number three brings together your mental, physical and spiritual energies and is a definite 'go get 'em' kinda number. Use the number three when you want to bring money to you quickly or seal a deal in record time.

No. 4 – A caring number which focuses on your emotions but also your creativity. It represents the four elements, the four compass directions and the seasons. Use this number to bring in the elements of earth, air, fire and water to help manifest your desires and wishes.

No. 5 – Number five brings changes, transformation and movement but it can be also bring about a bit of chaos. Good to work with for making quick changes in your finances but be wary of the chaotic energy!

No. 6 – Six is a masculine power number that brings security and responsibility. Definitely a number to use to keep your finances safe and secure.

No. 7 – Seven is the feminine power number that brings intuition and wisdom. A number to use when you want to put a wish or desire into action, very good in any kind of money spell.

No. 8 – Talk to me! Number eight is all about communication and messages but also material wealth and success. Excellent for all kinds of money, prosperity and abundance magic.

No. 9 – A transitional number that leads to completion and fulfilment of your project, wishes or desires. If you want to bring a deal or transition to a successful completion, then number nine is the one to use.

Days

Working your spell on a specific day of the week that is associated with prosperity can add a powerful punch of energy to it.

Thursday for abundance, finances, prosperity, and wealth
Sunday for prosperity, success, and wealth
Wednesday for fortune
Tuesday for success

Planets

Tying in your spell with the moon phase being in a certain planetary position can add power to the magic. You can also carve or write the planetary sign into your spell working.

Jupiter for abundance, prosperity, and wealth
Venus for good fortune, money, and success

Moon for manifesting and riches
Sun for prosperity
Mars for success

Zodiac Signs

Use your own zodiac sign within the spell to bring a personal connection or work your magic when the moon phase is in a specific zodiac sign.

Taurus for prosperity
Virgo for prosperity
Cancer for abundance
Leo for fast cash

Tarot Cards

This is a list of the cards that I often use in my money drawing spells. Each one reflects an aspect of prosperity, abundance or wealth. Of course, there are also cards that can be used in spell workings to help release debt or stop bad spending habits, I have included those here too. Use the ones that you feel most drawn to.

Abundance – The Empress, The Star, The World, Ace of Pentacles, Six of Pentacles, Nine of Pentacles, Ace of Cups.

Action/to set things in motion – The Chariot, The Empress, Ace of Wands, Eight of Wands.

Bad habits, to overcome: Strength, Temperance, Judgement, The World.

Balance – The Lovers, Justice, Temperance, Two of Swords, Four of Wands, Two of Cups.

Business prosperity – Three of Wands, The Sun, Ace of Pentacles.

Changes – Wheel of Fortune, The Magician, Hanged Man, Death, The Tower, Judgement, The World, Knight of Swords, Eight of Wands.

Employment – Justice, The Emperor, Judgement, Page of Wands, Two of Wands, Eight of Pentacles, Ace of Pentacles, Ace of Wands, Three of Wands, Four of Wands.

Goals – The Emperor, The Chariot, Strength.

Growth – The Empress, The Hermit.

Luck – The World, The Star, Wheel of Fortune.

New beginnings – The Fool, The Emperor, The World, The Chariot, The Hermit, Death, The Sun, Two of Pentacles, Ten of Swords, Ace of Wands, Knight of Wands, Four of Cups, Eight of Cups.

New business/project success – The Magician, The Sun, Ace of Wands, The Empress, Seven of Pentacles.

Opportunities – The Magician, Wheel of Fortune, The Devil, The Star, The World, Knight of Cups, Seven of Cups.

Potential – The Fool.

Prosperity and money – Wheel of Fortune, Ten of Pentacles, Knight of Pentacles, Page of Pentacles, Six of Pentacles, Ace of Pentacles, Two of Pentacles, Four of Pentacles, Queen of Pentacles.

Releasing – Hanged Man, Death, The Devil, The Tower, Four of Swords, Six of Swords.

Success – The Chariot, Wheel of Fortune, Justice, The Star, The Moon, The Sun, The World, Ace of Pentacles, Queen of Pentacles, King of Pentacles, Ace of Swords, Two of Swords, Six of Swords.

Extras

To boost your prosperity magic you can add other items into your spell working that represent money or abundance.

Coins are a good item to use in prosperity spells, as they literally represent money. I like to work with small silver coins because they bring in silver colour magic. Coins can be placed in front of a candle whilst working a spell; I recommend creating a circle of small coins around your candle. You could carve a slot and push a coin into the side of the candle; once the candle burns down and releases the coin, your spell is done. Alternatively, you could push a small coin into the base of your candle. Coins can be used as prosperity charms after a spell is finished; place the coin on your altar on in your purse.

Chocolate is a good representation of abundance and wealth. It can be incorporated by placing squares of chocolate in front of your candle.

Nuts bring positive magical energy in the form of abundance. They can be placed in front of your candle or arranged in a circle around it.

You could fold up currency notes and set them under the candle or in front of it but be mindful that they could catch flame or be ruined by the wax.

Disposing of Spells

Once your spell has been worked you will often be left with candle stubs, herbs and/or other items. Trust your intuition and how you feel they need to be disposed of. Herbs and natural items can be composted or buried. Some items can be burnt. Others you may need to just throw in the trash. Please don't bury anything that is not biodegradable.

About the Author

I am an English witch who has been walking the Pagan pathway for over thirty years. A working wife and mother who has been lucky enough to have had over 30 books published (so far), some of them becoming best sellers. My passion is to learn, I love to study and have done so from books, online resources, schools and wonderful mentors over the years and still continue to learn each and every day, but I have learnt the most from actually getting outside and doing it.

I like to laugh ... and eat cake...

It is my pleasure to give talks to pagan groups and co-run open rituals and workshops run by the Kitchen Witch Coven. I am also High Priestess of the Kitchen Witch Coven and an Elder at the online Kitchen Witch School of Natural Witchcraft. I am the host of the Pagan Portal Podcast.

A regular columnist with Fate & Fortune magazine, I also contribute articles to several magazines such as Pagan Dawn and Witchcraft & Wicca. You will find my regular ramblings on my own personal blog and YouTube channel.

My craft is a combination of old religion witchcraft, Wicca, hedge witchery, kitchen witchery and folk magic. My heart is that of an English Kitchen Witch.

It was my honour to be added to the Watkins 'Spiritual 100 List' for 2023.

www.rachelpatterson.co.uk
facebook.com/rachelpattersonbooks
www.kitchenwitchhearth.net
facebook.com/kitchenwitchuk
Email: HQ@kitchenwitchhearth.net

www.youtube.com/user/Kitchenwitchuk
www.instagram.com/racheltansypatterson

MY BOOKS

Kitchen Witchcraft Series

Spells & Charms
Garden Magic
Crystal Magic
The Element of Earth
The Element of Fire
The Element of Water

Pagan Portals

Kitchen Witchcraft
Hoodoo Folk Magic
Moon Magic
Meditation
The Cailleach
Animal Magic
Sun Magic
Triple Goddess
Gods & Goddesses of England
Dragon Magic
Sulis

Other Moon Books

The Art of Ritual
Beneath the Moon
Witchcraft ... into the Wilds
Grimoire of a Kitchen Witch
A Kitchen Witch's World of Magical Foods
A Kitchen Witch's World of Magical Plants & Herbs
Arc of the Goddess (co-written with Tracey Roberts)

Moon Books Gods & Goddesses Colouring Book (Patterson family)
Practically Pagan: An Alternative Guide to Cooking

Llewellyn
Curative Magic
A Witch for All Seasons: Spells, Rituals, Festivals, and Magic
Practical Candle Magic: Witchcraft with Wick & Wax

Solarus
Flower Magic Oracle Deck
Animal Dreaming Publishing
Magical Herbs Oracle Deck part of the Kitchen Witch series
Fenix Flames Publishing
Hedge Witch & the Art of Hedge Riding
Animal Dreaming Publishing
Kitchen Witchcraft Oracle Deck Series

MOON BOOKS

PAGANISM & SHAMANISM

What is Paganism? A religion, a spirituality, an alternative belief system, nature worship? You can find support for all these definitions (and many more) in dictionaries, encyclopaedias, and text books of religion, but subscribe to any one and the truth will evade you. Above all Paganism is a creative pursuit, an encounter with reality, an exploration of meaning and an expression of the soul. Druids, Heathens, Wiccans and others, all contribute their insights and literary riches to the Pagan tradition. Moon Books invites you to begin or to deepen your own encounter, right here, right now.

If you have enjoyed this book, why not tell other readers by posting a review on your preferred book site.

Bestsellers from Moon Books

Keeping Her Keys

An Introduction to Hekate's Modern Witchcraft

Cyndi Brannen

Blending Hekate, witchcraft and personal development together to create a powerful new magickal perspective.

Paperback: 978-1-78904-075-3 ebook 978-1-78904-076-0

Journey to the Dark Goddess

How to Return to Your Soul

Jane Meredith

Discover the powerful secrets of the Dark Goddess and transform your depression, grief and pain into healing and integration.

Paperback: 978-1-84694-677-6 ebook: 978-1-78099-223-5

Shamanic Reiki

Expanded Ways of Working with Universal Life Force Energy

Llyn Roberts, Robert Levy

Shamanism and Reiki are each powerful ways of healing; together, their power multiplies. Shamanic Reiki introduces techniques to help healers and Reiki practitioners tap ancient healing wisdom.

Paperback: 978-1-84694-037-8 ebook: 978-1-84694-650-9

Southern Cunning

Folkloric Witchcraft in the American South

Aaron Oberon

Modern witchcraft with a Southern flair, this book is a journey through the folklore of the American South and a look at the power these stories hold for modern witches.

Paperback: 978-1-78904-196-5 ebook: 978-1-78904-197-2

Bestsellers from Moon Books
Pagan Portals Series

The Morrigan
Meeting the Great Queens
Morgan Daimler
Ancient and enigmatic, the Morrigan reaches out to us. On shadowed wings and in raven's call, meet the ancient Irish goddess of war, battle, prophecy, death, sovereignty, and magic.
Paperback: 978-1-78279-833-0 ebook: 978-1-78279-834-7

The Awen Alone
Walking the Path of the Solitary Druid
Joanna van der Hoeven
An introductory guide for the solitary Druid, The Awen Alone will accompany you as you explore, and seek out your own place within the natural world.
Paperback: 978-1-78279-547-6 ebook: 978-1-78279-546-9

Moon Magic
Rachel Patterson
An introduction to working with the phases of the Moon, what they are and how to live in harmony with the lunar year and to utilise all the magical powers it provides.
Paperback: 978-1-78279-281-9 ebook: 978-1-78279-282-6

Hekate
A Devotional
Vivienne Moss
Hekate, Queen of Witches and the Shadow-Lands, haunts the pages of this devotional bringing magic and enchantment into your lives.
Paperback: 978-1-78535-161-7 ebook: 978-1-78535-162-4